NES Special Education

Mia O. Pang

This page is intentionally left blank.

ISBN/SKU: 978-1-0882-6667-0

This page is intentionally left blank.

Table of Content

This page is intentionally left blank.

Chapter 1 – Questions

QUESTION 1

Sarah, a 10-year-old student with Down syndrome, has been making slow progress in her academic and social skills. She often struggles to communicate effectively and has difficulty following multi-step instructions. In the classroom, she frequently becomes overwhelmed and anxious. As a special education teacher, what is the most appropriate approach to support Sarah's learning and emotional needs?

    A. Place Sarah in a mainstream classroom with minimal accommodations to encourage independence.

    B. Implement an Individualized Education Plan (IEP) tailored to her specific needs, focusing on communication and social skills development.

    C. Provide Sarah with extra time to complete assignments and assessments, so she can catch up with her peers.

    D. Organize occasional workshops for Sarah's parents to manage her anxiety and stress at home.

Answer:

QUESTION 2

Which characteristic is commonly associated with students diagnosed with Attention Deficit Hyperactivity Disorder (ADHD)?

    A. Exceptional organizational skills and time management.

    B. An intense focus on repetitive tasks.

    C. Impulsivity, inattention, and hyperactivity.

    D. High tolerance for changes in routines.

Answer:

QUESTION 3

Alex is a 14-year-old student with autism spectrum disorder (ASD). He has a strong interest in computer programming and excels in this area. However, he struggles with social interactions, has repetitive behaviors, and experiences sensory sensitivities. As a special education teacher, what is the best way to support Alex's strengths and address his challenges?

    A. Discourage Alex's interest in computer programming to focus on improving his social interactions.

    B. Ignore his repetitive behaviors to avoid causing additional stress.

    C. Develop a social skills group to help him improve his interaction with peers.

    D. Enroll Alex in extracurricular activities to expose him to different sensory experiences.

Answer:

QUESTION 4

Which characteristic is common among students with specific learning disabilities?

    A. Advanced reading and writing skills compared to their peers.

    B. Consistently high academic performance across all subjects.

    C. Difficulty with one or more academic skills despite having average to above-average intelligence.

    D. Exceptional verbal communication but limited nonverbal communication.

Answer:

QUESTION 5

Mark is a 12-year-old student with dyslexia. He often struggles with reading and spelling tasks, leading to frustration and a decline in his self-confidence. Despite these challenges, Mark is highly creative and excels in arts and crafts activities. As a special education teacher, what is the most effective way to support Mark's learning and boost his self-esteem?

    A. Assign extra reading and spelling practice to improve his skills gradually.
    B. Enroll Mark in a specialized dyslexia school to focus solely on his reading difficulties.
    C. Provide opportunities for Mark to showcase his creativity through arts-related projects.
    D. Ignore his reading difficulties and concentrate solely on his artistic abilities.

Answer:

QUESTION 6

Jenny, a 15-year-old student with cerebral palsy, is highly motivated to participate in physical education classes with her peers. However, she faces significant mobility challenges and requires the use of a wheelchair for mobility. As a special education teacher, what is the most appropriate approach to ensure Jenny's inclusion and active participation in physical education activities?

    A. Assign an assistant to accompany Jenny during physical education classes and complete tasks on her behalf.
    B. Excuse Jenny from physical education classes to avoid any potential embarrassment or discomfort.
    C. Modify physical education activities to accommodate Jenny's needs and provide adaptive equipment.
    D. Encourage Jenny to observe physical education classes from the sidelines to avoid any risks.

Answer:

QUESTION 7

What is one potential implication of having a nonverbal learning disability (NVLD) for social relationships?

    A. Difficulty with math-related concepts and tasks.
    B. Trouble understanding and interpreting nonverbal cues and body language.
    C. Challenges in expressing emotions and feelings verbally.
    D. Inability to retain and recall factual information accurately.

Answer:

QUESTION 8

Mark, an 18-year-old with autism spectrum disorder (ASD), is preparing to transition from high school to post-secondary education. He excels in academics and is passionate about computer programming. However, he often experiences sensory overload in crowded or noisy environments. As a special education teacher, what should you prioritize to support Mark's transition to post-secondary education?

    A. Encourage Mark to consider online courses to minimize exposure to sensory overload.
    B. Discourage Mark from pursuing post-secondary education due to potential challenges.
    C. Focus solely on academic preparations and neglect the sensory challenges Mark faces.
    D. Collaborate with post-secondary institutions to provide appropriate accommodations for Mark's sensory needs.

Answer:

QUESTION 9

What is a potential implication of having a specific learning disability (SLD) in the context of employment?

A. Difficulty with social interactions, leading to isolation in the workplace.
B. Limited ability to use assistive technology effectively.
C. Inability to handle criticism and feedback from supervisors.
D. Challenges in understanding and following written or verbal instructions accurately.

Answer:

QUESTION 10

Linda, a 20-year-old student with a visual impairment, is interested in pursuing independent living after completing her education. She has demonstrated strong organizational and daily living skills. However, she faces challenges with accessing written information. As a special education teacher, what is the most effective way to empower Linda for independent living?

A. Discourage Linda from pursuing independent living due to her visual impairment.
B. Provide Linda with audio-based resources and technologies to access information.
C. Focus solely on her organizational and daily living skills and ignore the reading challenges.
D. Assign a personal assistant to handle all reading-related tasks for Linda.

Answer:

QUESTION 11

Which of the following best represents a characteristic of typical cognitive development in early childhood?

A. Logical reasoning and abstract thinking skills develop rapidly.
B. Memory capabilities are fully matured.
C. Symbolic play and imaginative thinking become less prominent.
D. Egocentrism and difficulty understanding others' perspectives decrease.

Answer:

QUESTION 12

You are working with a 5-year-old child who has atypical speech and language development. The child is mostly nonverbal and relies on gestures and single-word utterances to communicate basic needs. Which of the following communication strategies would be most appropriate to support this child's language development?

A. Encouraging the child to speak in full sentences during structured activities.
B. Using flashcards and worksheets to teach new vocabulary.
C. Implementing augmentative and alternative communication (AAC) tools, such as picture symbols or communication devices.
D. Correcting the child's pronunciation and grammar errors frequently.

Answer:

QUESTION 13

Which of the following statements best describes a characteristic of atypical social/emotional development in adolescence?

    A. A typical adolescent tends to exhibit consistent and stable moods.
    B. A typical adolescent seeks less independence from their caregivers.
    C. A typical adolescent may experience heightened peer pressure and conformity.
    D. A typical adolescent's self-identity remains unchallenged during this period.

Answer:

QUESTION 14

You are working with a 9-year-old child who demonstrates typical physical development. The child is having difficulty maintaining attention during classroom activities and frequently fidgets, taps their feet, and squirms in their seat. They often interrupt others and struggle to wait their turn. The child's teacher reports these behaviors have been present for at least six months and are impacting their academic performance and social interactions. Based on this case study, what condition might be the best explanation for the child's difficulties?

    A. Specific learning disability in reading.
    B. Oppositional defiant disorder (ODD).
    C. Attention-deficit/hyperactivity disorder (ADHD).
    D. Autism spectrum disorder (ASD).

Answer:

QUESTION 15

You are working with a student who has a specific learning disability and also experiences seizures. The student's seizures are characterized by brief periods of staring and subtle body movements. Which of the following medication options is most appropriate for managing this student's seizures while considering their specific learning disability?

    A. Methylphenidate (Ritalin) to improve attention and focus.
    B. Fluoxetine (Prozac) to address anxiety and mood swings.
    C. Levetiracetam (Keppra) for seizure control.
    D. Guanfacine (Intuniv) for impulsivity and hyperactivity.

Answer:

QUESTION 16

Which of the following statements about medication administration in the school setting for students with disabilities is correct?

    A. School staff, including teachers, can administer prescription medications without any special training or authorization.
    B. Over-the-counter medications can be given to students with disabilities without parental consent.
    C. Medication administration should be documented accurately and kept confidential.
    D. Students with disabilities can self-administer any medications without supervision.

Answer:

QUESTION 17

You are working with a student who has cerebral palsy and experiences muscle spasticity, leading to difficulties with mobility. The student's physical therapist recommends medication to manage spasticity. Which of the following medication options is most appropriate for this student's condition?

    A. Risperidone (Risperdal) for behavioral management.
    B. Dextroamphetamine (Adderall) to improve alertness and focus.
    C. Baclofen (Lioresal) for muscle spasticity.
    D. Sertraline (Zoloft) for social anxiety.

Answer:

QUESTION 18

Which of the following best describes the role of a special education teacher regarding medication administration for students with disabilities?

    A. The special education teacher is responsible for diagnosing medical conditions and prescribing appropriate medications.
    B. The special education teacher should determine the dosage and frequency of medications for students with disabilities.
    C. The special education teacher collaborates with parents, medical professionals, and school staff to ensure safe and proper medication administration.
    D. The special education teacher is solely responsible for administering medications to students with disabilities.

Answer:

QUESTION 19

Sarah is a 10-year-old student with Down syndrome. She enjoys drawing and coloring during her free time. In the classroom, she often has difficulty understanding complex math problems and needs additional support. What best describes Sarah's disability and her strengths?

    A. Intellectual Disability; Strength in Artistic Abilities
    B. Specific Learning Disability; Strength in Artistic Abilities
    C. Emotional and Behavioral Disorder; Strength in Artistic Abilities
    D. Speech and Language Impairment; Strength in Artistic Abilities

Answer:

QUESTION 20

Which disability category involves a persistent difficulty in reading and/or writing, despite adequate instruction and average intelligence?

    A. Intellectual Disability
    B. Autism Spectrum Disorder
    C. Specific Learning Disability
    D. Speech and Language Impairment

Answer:

QUESTION 21

Jason is a 7-year-old student with autism. He becomes highly agitated and displays aggressive behavior when there is a change in the classroom routine or environment. Which type of disability does Jason have, and what is the primary trigger for his agitated and aggressive behavior?

   A.   Emotional and Behavioral Disorder; Sensory Overload
   B.   Specific Learning Disability; Social Anxiety
   C.   Autism Spectrum Disorder; Sensory Overload
   D.   Intellectual Disability; Social Anxiety

Answer:

QUESTION 22

Which disability is primarily characterized by difficulties in communication, such as speech articulation and language comprehension?

   A.   Emotional and Behavioral Disorder
   B.   Intellectual Disability
   C.   Speech and Language Impairment
   D.   Autism Spectrum Disorder

Answer:

QUESTION 23

Emma is a 12-year-old student with a specific learning disability. She often struggles to express herself in writing and frequently misspells words. Which area should the special education teacher focus on to support Emma's needs?

   A.   Math Problem Solving
   B.   Artistic Expression
   C.   Reading Comprehension
   D.   Written Expression

Answer:

QUESTION 24

Sarah is a 10-year-old student with a specific learning disability in reading. Despite receiving appropriate interventions, she continues to struggle with decoding and comprehension. During reading sessions, she often displays signs of frustration, avoids reading tasks, and experiences difficulty in retaining information. As a special education teacher, what is the most appropriate next step to support Sarah's learning?

   A.   Provide more challenging reading materials to encourage her to work harder.
   B.   Modify the reading curriculum to focus exclusively on her interests.
   C.   Collaborate with the school's speech therapist to address potential language processing issues.
   D.   Assign extra homework to reinforce reading skills outside of school hours.

Answer:

QUESTION 25

Which factor is most likely to have a significant impact on the daily living skills development of students with intellectual disabilities?

   A. Socioeconomic status
   B. Genetic factors
   C. Access to advanced technology
   D. Individualized educational plans

Answer:

QESTION 26

Jason is a 7-year-old student with autism spectrum disorder (ASD). He has shown great interest in music and responds positively to it during therapy sessions. As a special education teacher, what is the most appropriate strategy to use music to support Jason's learning and development?

   A. Use music as a reward for completing non-preferred tasks.
   B. Incorporate music into various learning activities across the curriculum.
   C. Restrict Jason's exposure to music to prevent sensory overload.
   D. Use music only during music therapy sessions and not in other settings.

Answer:

QUESTION 27

Which of the following best represents an inclusive approach when planning classroom activities for students with diverse disabilities?

   A. Assigning separate activities based on each student's specific disability.
   B. Designing activities that cater only to the needs of neurotypical students.
   C. Implementing activities with minimal adaptations for students with disabilities.
   D. Creating activities that accommodate the needs of all students, regardless of their abilities.

Answer:

QUESTION 28

Emma is a 15-year-old student with attention deficit hyperactivity disorder (ADHD). She often struggles with time management and maintaining focus during class lectures and assignments. As a special education teacher, what is the most appropriate accommodation to support Emma's learning?

   A. Reducing her workload to alleviate stress and pressure.
   B. Assigning a peer buddy to constantly remind her of important deadlines.
   C. Providing written or visual cues to help her stay on track with time management.
   D. Allowing her to skip class lectures to study independently at her own pace.

Answer:

QUESTION 29

Alex is a 12-year-old student with a physical disability that affects his fine motor skills. He struggles with writing and often experiences frustration during class activities that involve handwriting. As a special education teacher, what is the most appropriate accommodation to support Alex's writing tasks?

    A. Providing a scribe to write down his thoughts during assessments.
    B. Excusing him from all writing activities to avoid frustration.
    C. Assigning additional writing homework to improve his skills.
    D. Encouraging him to use a computer for all writing tasks.

Answer:

QUESTION 30

Which factor is most likely to impact the development of social skills in students with autism spectrum disorder (ASD)?

    A. Exposure to social skills training programs.
    B. Engagement in solitary play activities.
    C. Limited access to technology devices.
    D. High cognitive abilities.

Answer:

QUESTION 31

Maria is a 9-year-old student with a specific learning disability in mathematics. She struggles with understanding mathematical concepts and often performs below grade level. Despite receiving targeted interventions, her progress has been slow. As a special education teacher, what is the most appropriate step to support Maria's learning?

    A. Advancing her to the next grade level in mathematics to challenge her.
    B. Focusing solely on her strengths in other subjects to build confidence.
    C. Conducting a comprehensive evaluation to identify specific areas of difficulty.
    D. Assigning extra homework in mathematics to improve her skills.

Answer:

QUESTION 32

When adapting classroom materials for students with visual impairments, what is the most effective approach to ensure accessibility?

    A. Using smaller fonts to fit more content on a page.
    B. Providing audio recordings of all classroom materials.
    C. Using tactile graphics and braille alongside printed text.
    D. Reducing the amount of written content to simplify materials.

Answer:

QUESTION 33

Which of the following is a critical factor for promoting self-determination in students with disabilities?

   A. Providing constant assistance to complete tasks.
   B. Making decisions for the students to avoid potential mistakes.
   C. Allowing students to take an active role in setting their goals.
   D. Shielding students from challenging situations to reduce stress.

Answer:

QUESTION 34

Sarah is a 10-year-old student with a learning disability. Her parents are involved in her education and regularly attend parent-teacher conferences. However, they are hesitant to join any school committees or volunteer for school events due to their busy work schedules. What is the best way for a special education teacher to involve Sarah's parents in her learning and development?

   A. Encourage Sarah's parents to join the school's Parent-Teacher Association (PTA) to actively engage in school decision-making.
   B. Suggest Sarah's parents participate in regular parent-teacher conferences to stay updated on her progress.
   C. Recommend Sarah's parents to volunteer at school events to foster a sense of community involvement.
   D. Arrange a convenient alternative communication method, such as emails or virtual meetings, to accommodate Sarah's parents' busy schedules.

Answer:

QUESTION 35

David is an 8-year-old student with autism spectrum disorder. His family comes from a culturally diverse background and follows unique traditions and customs. How can a special education teacher effectively support David's development and learning, taking his cultural background into account?

   A. Implement individualized teaching strategies exclusively based on David's cultural preferences and beliefs.
   B. Collaborate with the school's multicultural liaison to understand David's cultural background better.
   C. Encourage David's family to conform to the school's practices to create a consistent learning environment.
   D. Modify the curriculum entirely to include only culturally relevant content for David.

Answer:

QUESTION 36

Lily is a 12-year-old student with a specific learning disability. Her parents are actively involved in her school life and frequently communicate with the teacher. However, Lily is often hesitant to share her academic challenges with her parents, fearing it may disappoint them. What can a special education teacher do to encourage open communication between Lily and her parents about her academic struggles?

   A. Arrange regular parent-teacher conferences to discuss Lily's challenges and progress.
   B. Provide Lily with additional academic support outside of class to improve her performance.
   C. Establish a safe and supportive environment in the classroom where students can share their concerns.
   D. Offer rewards to students like Lily for sharing their academic difficulties with their parents.

Answer:

QUESTION 37

Mark is an 11-year-old student with attention-deficit/hyperactivity disorder (ADHD). His parents are highly involved in his education and are interested in collaborating with the school to enhance his learning experience. How can a special education teacher best engage Mark's parents in his educational journey?

    A. Assign them specific tasks during school events to actively involve them in school activities.

    B. Provide them with informative resources and articles about ADHD to educate them further.

    C. Encourage them to participate in parent-teacher conferences and share their suggestions.

    D. Invite them to join the school's general Parent-Teacher Association (PTA) meetings.

Answer:

QUESTION 38

Emma is a 7-year-old student with a visual impairment. Her parents are actively involved in her education and regularly attend meetings with the school's Individualized Education Plan (IEP) team. What can a special education teacher do to further involve Emma's parents in her development and learning?

    A. Encourage Emma's parents to participate in school fundraising events to support students with disabilities.

    B. Provide Emma's parents with resources about visual impairment and strategies to support her at home.

    C. Recommend Emma's parents to take on leadership roles within the school's Parent-Teacher Association (PTA).

    D. Organize a separate support group exclusively for parents of visually impaired students.

Answer:

QUESTION 39

Ethan is a 9-year-old student with autism spectrum disorder (ASD). His family comes from a culturally diverse background and speaks English as a second language. How can a special education teacher support Ethan's family in their involvement with his education?

    A. Provide Ethan's family with translated materials and interpreters during school events.

    B. Encourage Ethan's family to prioritize English language learning to improve communication.

    C. Assign a peer buddy to Ethan from a similar cultural background to assist with language barriers.

    D. Suggest that Ethan's family seek specialized autism training to better understand his needs.

Answer:

QUESTION 40

James is a 14-year-old student with dyslexia. His parents are actively involved in advocating for his educational rights and support. What can a special education teacher do to collaborate effectively with James's parents in his educational journey?

    A. Encourage James's parents to consider alternative schooling options that specialize in dyslexia support.

    B. Provide James's parents with regular progress reports and academic assessments.

    C. Organize a meeting with James's parents to discuss potential labeling of his learning disability.

    D. Refer James's parents to counseling services to cope with the challenges of raising a child with dyslexia.

Answer:

QUESTION 41

Mia is a 6-year-old student with attention-deficit/hyperactivity disorder (ADHD). Her parents are supportive of her education but express concerns about her interactions with peers. How can a special education teacher involve Mia's parents in improving her social interactions at school?

    A. Encourage Mia's parents to enroll her in extracurricular activities to develop social skills.

    B. Provide Mia's parents with books and articles on ADHD management at home.

    C. Schedule regular parent-teacher conferences to discuss Mia's peer interactions.

    D. Offer Mia's parents rewards for encouraging her to make new friends at school.

Answer:

QUESTION 42

You are a special education teacher working with a student who has a learning disability in reading. During the assessment process, the student demonstrates difficulty decoding unfamiliar words and exhibits slow and inaccurate reading. Which intervention strategy would be most appropriate for this student?

    A. Providing additional math instruction to strengthen overall academic performance.

    B. Implementing a multisensory reading program that focuses on phonics and decoding skills.

    C. Increasing the amount of time spent on physical education to improve overall cognitive functioning.

    D. Enrolling the student in an art class to encourage creativity and self-expression.

Answer:

QUESTION 43

What is the primary purpose of conducting ongoing assessments for students in special education programs?

    A. To meet state-mandated testing requirements.

    B. To compare students' performance with their peers in regular education classrooms.

    C. To monitor progress, make instructional decisions, and adjust teaching strategies.

    D. To determine the eligibility of students for special education services.

Answer:

QUESTION 44

You are a special education teacher working with a student who has autism spectrum disorder (ASD). The student displays repetitive behaviors and struggles with social communication. Which assessment tool would be most appropriate to gather information about the student's specific communication and social interaction challenges?

    A. Woodcock-Johnson Tests of Achievement (WJTA).

    B. Vineland Adaptive Behavior Scales (Vineland-3).

    C. Peabody Picture Vocabulary Test (PPVT-5).

    D. Childhood Autism Rating Scale (CARS).

Answer:

QUESTION 45

When designing an Individualized Education Program (IEP) for a student with disabilities, who should be actively involved in the process?

- A. School administrators and the special education teacher only.
- B. The special education teacher and general education teacher only.
- C. The student's parents or guardians, general education teacher, and relevant specialists.
- D. The school psychologist and the student's peers.

Answer:

QUESTION 46

Which of the following statements best describes the purpose of formative assessment in special education?

- A. To evaluate the overall effectiveness of the special education program.
- B. To determine a student's eligibility for special education services.
- C. To measure a student's academic performance at the end of the school year.
- D. To provide ongoing feedback and inform instructional decisions during the learning process.

Answer:

QUESTION 47

You are a special education teacher working with a student who has a specific learning disability in mathematics. After conducting assessments, you notice that the student struggles with understanding fractions and often confuses different operations involving fractions. Which instructional approach would be most effective in addressing this student's needs?

- A. Providing advanced math worksheets to challenge the student's understanding of fractions.
- B. Focusing on other math topics until the student demonstrates improved comprehension of fractions.
- C. Implementing a systematic, research-based intervention targeting the understanding of fractions.
- D. Assigning extra homework to reinforce concepts and encourage more practice with fractions.

Answer:

QUESTION 48

Which of the following is the most appropriate way for a special education teacher to use formative assessment data?

- A. As a one-time evaluation to determine a student's overall academic performance.
- B. To compare a student's performance with the rest of the class.
- C. To identify a student's strengths and weaknesses and adjust instruction accordingly.
- D. As the sole basis for determining a student's eligibility for special education services.

Answer:

QUESTION 49

A special education teacher is working with a student who has attention deficit hyperactivity disorder (ADHD) and exhibits impulsive behavior in the classroom. The student often interrupts others during discussions and has difficulty waiting for their turn. Which assessment tool would be most helpful in gathering data to address the student's impulsive behavior?

- A. Behavior Assessment System for Children (BASC-3).
- B. Woodcock-Johnson Tests of Achievement (WJTA).
- C. Wechsler Intelligence Scale for Children (WISC-V).
- D. Peabody Picture Vocabulary Test (PPVT-5).

Answer:

QUESTION 50

After conducting an assessment on a student with autism spectrum disorder (ASD), you have collected data on their communication skills, sensory processing, and adaptive behaviors. What is the most appropriate next step for a special education teacher to take based on this data?

- A. Focus solely on addressing communication skills through speech therapy.
- B. Review the assessment data with the parents and involve them in creating a personalized education plan.
- C. Disregard the data and rely on personal observations to plan instruction for the student.
- D. Compare the student's performance with neurotypical peers to set appropriate academic goals.

Answer:

QUESTION 51

When analyzing assessment data for a student with learning disabilities, you notice a significant discrepancy between the student's cognitive abilities and academic achievement. What does this discrepancy suggest, and what should be the appropriate next step for the special education teacher?

- A. The student may have a sensory processing disorder; refer the student for occupational therapy.
- B. The student may be exhibiting attention difficulties; refer the student for a comprehensive evaluation.
- C. The student's cognitive abilities are superior, and they should be placed in advanced academic programs.
- D. The student may have a specific learning disability; consider appropriate academic interventions.

Answer:

QUESTION 52

You are a special education teacher preparing to develop an Individualized Education Program (IEP) for a student with a specific learning disability in written expression. Which criterion is most crucial in determining appropriate goals and objectives for this student's IEP?

- A. The student's age and grade level in comparison to their peers.
- B. The specific learning disability category identified in the evaluation report.
- C. The student's strengths, weaknesses, and present levels of academic performance.
- D. The teacher's preferred instructional methods and materials.

Answer:

QUESTION 53

What is the primary purpose of including measurable goals and objectives in an Individualized Education Program (IEP) or other individualized plans?

    A. To align with state standards and curriculum guidelines.
    B. To provide flexibility in instructional approaches for teachers.
    C. To ensure parents are actively involved in the educational process.
    D. To track the student's progress and determine the effectiveness of interventions.

Answer:

QUESTION 54

A special education teacher is developing an Individualized Education Program (IEP) for a student with autism spectrum disorder (ASD) who struggles with social interactions and communication. Which strategy should the teacher consider when determining appropriate social and communication goals for the student's IEP?

    A. Assigning the student a peer buddy to assist with social interactions during lunch and recess.
    B. Providing the student with more time for independent academic work to avoid social situations.
    C. Incorporating the use of visual supports and social stories to improve social understanding.
    D. Allowing the student to participate only in individual therapy sessions to avoid group settings.

Answer:

QUESTION 55

When determining annual goals for an Individualized Education Program (IEP) or other individualized plans, what is the best practice for making the goals attainable and meaningful for the student?

    A. Developing goals based solely on the student's interests and preferences.
    B. Setting goals that are challenging but aligned with the student's present levels of performance.
    C. Assigning goals that align with the teacher's preferred methods of instruction.
    D. Using the same goals for all students in the same grade level.

Answer:

QUESTION 56

Which team members should be actively involved in the development of an Individualized Education Program (IEP) or other individualized plans for a student with disabilities?

    A. Only the special education teacher and school principal.
    B. The student's parents or guardians, general education teacher, and relevant specialists.
    C. The student's classmates and close friends.
    D. The school psychologist and other administrators.

Answer:

QUESTION 57

Mr. Johnson, a special education teacher, is assessing a student with learning disabilities to determine their reading level. He wants to use an informal assessment that includes asking the student to read a passage and answer comprehension questions orally. However, the student has speech difficulties and might feel uncomfortable answering questions verbally. What should Mr. Johnson do?

    A. Proceed with the planned informal assessment since it aligns with the reading level goal.
    B. Modify the informal assessment by providing the student with written comprehension questions to answer.
    C. Select a different informal assessment focusing on visual cues and eliminate verbal responses.
    D. Design a completely new assessment format focusing on the student's interests and strengths.

Answer:

QUESTION 58

As a special education teacher, you are using a standardized test to assess your students' mathematical abilities. However, you notice that one of your students, who has visual impairments, struggles to read the test questions. What should you do to address this situation?

    A. Allow the student extra time to complete the standardized test.
    B. Provide the student with an audio version of the standardized test.
    C. Request a different type of standardized test for the visually impaired student.
    D. Provide the student with a different assessment altogether, such as a performance-based evaluation.

Answer:

QUESTION 59

A special education teacher is assessing a student's writing skills using a standardized writing test. The test results indicate that the student is performing below grade level. To better understand the student's specific writing difficulties, what should the teacher do next?

    A. Design a new writing test with simpler prompts to re-assess the student's skills.
    B. Modify the existing standardized test by reducing the number of writing prompts.
    C. Use an informal writing assessment to gather more detailed information about the student's writing abilities.
    D. Select a different standardized test that focuses more on grammar and spelling.

Answer:

QUESTION 60

Ms. Smith is a special education teacher assessing a student with attention deficit hyperactivity disorder (ADHD) for their mathematical abilities. During the assessment, the student appears restless, has difficulty focusing, and struggles to complete written tasks within the given time. What modification should Ms. Smith consider to address these challenges?

    A. Providing additional breaks during the assessment to allow the student to move around.
    B. Shortening the assessment to reduce the number of questions and written tasks.
    C. Changing the assessment format to focus on oral questioning and responses.
    D. Eliminating the assessment for the student due to their ADHD challenges.

Answer:

QUESTION 61

A special education teacher is assessing a student with autism spectrum disorder (ASD) to evaluate their reading comprehension skills. The student exhibits difficulty understanding and responding to written text. What approach should the teacher take to effectively assess the student's reading comprehension?

    A. Use a visual-based reading assessment that relies on picture cues and illustrations.
    B. Provide the student with a simplified version of the reading text for comprehension assessment.
    C. Modify the assessment to focus solely on decoding skills rather than comprehension.
    D. Use an interactive reading assessment with audio support to aid the student's understanding.

Answer:

QUESTION 62

Ms. Adams is a special education teacher creating an individualized education program (IEP) for a student with learning disabilities. The student struggles with reading comprehension and written expression. What should Ms. Adams do to develop an effective IEP for the student?

    A. Focus the IEP on improving the student's reading comprehension skills only.
    B. Develop goals that align with the student's grade-level academic standards.
    C. Implement a one-size-fits-all approach for the student's learning needs.
    D. Include specific and measurable goals to address both reading comprehension and written expression.

Answer:

QUESTION 63

When monitoring the progress of an individualized program for a student with intellectual disabilities, what data should a special education teacher collect to make informed decisions?

    A. Only academic test scores and grades from mainstream classroom assignments.
    B. Anecdotal notes on the student's behavior in the special education classroom.
    C. Data related to the student's individualized goals and objectives.
    D. Information gathered solely from parent-teacher conferences.

Answer:

QUESTION 64

Mr. Rodriguez is a special education teacher responsible for implementing an individualized behavior intervention plan (BIP) for a student with emotional and behavioral disorders. The student's challenging behavior occurs most frequently during mathematics class. What should Mr. Rodriguez do to address this issue?

    A. Implement the BIP consistently across all subjects, including mathematics.
    B. Modify the mathematics curriculum to remove any challenging components.
    C. Observe the student during mathematics class to identify specific triggers.
    D. Suspend the BIP during mathematics class to avoid causing further distress.

Answer:

QUESTION 65

When developing an individualized program for a student with autism spectrum disorder (ASD), what is the significance of considering the student's interests and strengths?

    A. It helps in identifying areas of deficit that need to be addressed first.
    B. It ensures that the program is challenging enough to push the student's limits.
    C. It enhances the student's motivation and engagement in learning activities.
    D. It allows the teacher to avoid any modifications to the curriculum.

Answer:

QUESTION 66

As a special education teacher, how can you involve parents or guardians in the development and implementation of an individualized program for their child?

    A. Provide parents with a list of tasks they need to complete independently.
    B. Request parents to oversee all assessments and data collection.
    C. Schedule regular meetings to discuss the student's progress and goals collaboratively.
    D. Limit parents' involvement to ensure professional autonomy.

Answer:

QUESTION 67

Ms. Johnson, a special education teacher, is working with a student with specific learning disabilities. The student has made significant progress with appropriate supports in the general education classroom, but occasionally struggles to keep up with the pace of the class. What should Ms. Johnson do to enhance the student's integration into the general education program?

    A. Recommend moving the student to a self-contained special education classroom.
    B. Provide the student with a modified curriculum to match their pace.
    C. Collaborate with the general education teacher to implement targeted accommodations.
    D. Suggest skipping certain subjects to reduce the student's workload.

Answer:

QUESTION 68

A special education teacher is working with a student with emotional and behavioral disorders who has difficulty maintaining appropriate behavior in a mainstream classroom setting. The student's disruptions are occasionally disruptive to the learning of other students. What would be the most appropriate placement to consider for this student?

    A. An inclusion classroom with support from a behavior interventionist.
    B. A self-contained special education classroom with a smaller student-to-teacher ratio.
    C. A gifted and talented program with advanced academic challenges.
    D. A regular mainstream classroom without any additional support.

Answer:

QUESTION 69

When planning the continuum of services for students with disabilities, what should a special education teacher consider?

    A. The availability of extracurricular activities in each program placement.
    B. The potential budgetary impact of each program placement on the school.
    C. The specific needs and strengths of the students with disabilities.
    D. The preference of the general education teachers involved.

Answer:

QUESTION 70

Mr. Davis is a special education teacher responsible for a group of students with different disabilities. He wants to promote inclusion and collaboration among his students. What strategy could he use to enhance integration within the group?

    A. Group students based on their disability type to facilitate targeted support.
    B. Designate a student leader to guide and instruct the others during group activities.
    C. Encourage regular group discussions and activities that foster teamwork and empathy.
    D. Provide each student with individual tasks to prevent potential conflicts.

Answer:

QUESTION 71

A special education teacher is developing an individualized plan for a student with physical disabilities to support their integration into the general education program. The student uses a wheelchair and requires assistance with mobility. What state-approved support should the teacher consider to enhance the student's integration?

    A. Providing the student with a personal aide for all classroom activities.
    B. Implementing a curriculum specifically designed for students with physical disabilities.
    C. Ensuring all classroom materials are available in audio format for the student.
    D. Installing ramps and other accessibility features in the classroom and school premises.

Answer:

QUESTION 72

Which of the following assessment types is best suited for gathering in-depth information about a special education student's specific skills, strengths, and weaknesses in a particular area?

    A. Standardized test
    B. Curriculum-based assessment
    C. Criterion-referenced test
    D. Norm-referenced test

Answer:

QUESTION 73

Mrs. Adams is a special education teacher assessing a student with learning disabilities. She wants to assess the student's reading comprehension by having the student read a passage and answer questions orally. However, the student has difficulty with expressive language and becomes anxious during oral assessments. What type of alternative assessment would be most appropriate for Mrs. Adams to use?

A. Performance-based assessment
B. Portfolio assessment
C. Self-assessment
D. Informal reading inventory

Answer:

QUESTION 74

Which of the following assessment types is primarily used to compare a student's performance to that of their peers

A. Standardized test
B. Criterion-referenced test
C. Performance-based assessment
D. Formative assessment

Answer:

QUESTION 75

Mr. Johnson, a special education teacher, is conducting an informal assessment of a student's math skills. He observes the student during math activities and notes their performance. Which of the following types of informal assessments is Mr. Johnson using?

A. Running record
B. Anecdotal record
C. Self-assessment
D. Likert scale

Answer:

QUESTION 76

Mrs. Ramirez is a special education teacher working with a student who has limited communication abilities and requires an alternative means of assessment. She wants to assess the student's understanding of various science concepts. What type of alternative assessment would be most appropriate for Mrs. Ramirez to use?

A. Rubric-based assessment
B. Adaptive assessment
C. Dynamic assessment
D. Augmentative and Alternative Communication (AAC)-based assessment

Answer:

QUESTION 77

Ms. Anderson, a special education teacher, notices that a student in her class is struggling with reading comprehension and is falling behind academically. After conducting initial screenings and interventions, there are still concerns about the student's progress. What should be the next step for Ms. Anderson?

A. Refer the student for a comprehensive evaluation to determine eligibility for special education services.
B. Continue with the current interventions and wait for the student to catch up.
C. Conduct a prereferral intervention plan to address the student's reading comprehension difficulties.
D. Transfer the student to a different classroom with more academic support.

Answer:

QUESTION 78

Which of the following best defines a prereferral intervention process in a school setting?

A. A formal assessment procedure used to identify students with disabilities.
B. The process of referring a student to an outside agency for specialized services.
C. A collaborative approach to address a student's academic or behavioral difficulties within the general education setting before initiating a formal special education evaluation.
D. A process to determine if a student is eligible for gifted and talented programs.

Answer:

QUESTION 79

As a special education teacher, what is the primary purpose of conducting a screening process for students?

A. To determine if a student is eligible for gifted and talented programs.
B. To identify students who may be at risk for academic or behavioral difficulties.
C. To diagnose specific learning disabilities in students.
D. To assess the overall intelligence level of students.

Answer:

QUESTION 80

Which of the following is an essential component of a referral process for special education evaluation?

A. Obtaining consent from the parents or legal guardians of the student.
B. Conducting a comprehensive psychological evaluation.
C. Administering a series of standardized tests to the student.
D. Requesting input from other teachers in the school.

Answer:

QUESTION 81

Ms. Hernandez, a special education teacher, receives a referral for a new student, Daniel, who is experiencing academic challenges in a general education classroom. Daniel's teacher reports concerns about his reading and writing skills. What is the most appropriate initial step for Ms. Hernandez to take?

    A. Conduct a comprehensive evaluation of Daniel's academic abilities.

    B. Request Daniel's previous school records to gain insight into his academic history.

    C. Observe Daniel in the general education classroom to assess his behavior.

    D. Implement a prereferral intervention plan to support Daniel's reading and writing skills.

Answer:

QUESTION 82

Mr. Davis, a special education teacher, is working with a group of students with disabilities who struggle with organizational skills and time management. He wants to integrate strategies to help them improve these skills while addressing academic content. What approach should Mr. Davis use to best meet the students' needs?

    A. Implement a reward system to motivate students to improve their organizational skills.

    B. Develop a separate life skills curriculum to address organizational and time management skills.

    C. Incorporate visual schedules and checklists into the academic curriculum to support organization and time management.

    D. Assign additional homework to practice time management outside of regular classwork.

Answer:

QUESTION 83

When prioritizing areas of the general curriculum for students with disabilities, which of the following should be the primary consideration for special education teachers?

    A. Identifying areas that align with the students' strengths and interests.

    B. Focusing on areas that are required for standardized testing.

    C. Emphasizing areas that are most heavily covered in textbooks and instructional materials.

    D. Choosing areas that require the least amount of modifications and accommodations.

Answer:

QUESTION 84

Ms. Robinson is a special education teacher working with a student who has significant physical disabilities that limit their ability to write with traditional tools. Which assistive technology would best support the student's participation in written assignments?

    A. Voice recognition software

    B. Digital textbooks

    C. Interactive whiteboards

    D. Online research databases

Answer: A

Explanation: Voice recognition software would be the most appropriate assistive technology to support the student's participation in written assignments. This technology allows the student to dictate their responses, and the software converts their speech into text. It can significantly enhance the student's ability to complete written tasks independently and effectively, despite their physical limitations.

QUESTION 85

As a special education teacher, how can you effectively integrate affective and social skills with academic curricula?

    A.   Dedicate a separate lesson for teaching affective and social skills outside of academic time.
    B.   Embed social skill development within academic lessons and activities.
    C.   Offer counseling sessions to students to address affective and social challenges.
    D.   Assign students to peer-tutor each other to develop affective and social skills.

Answer:

QUESTION 86

When incorporating instructional and assistive technology into students' educational programs, what should be the primary consideration for special education teachers?

    A.   Selecting the most advanced and cutting-edge technology available.
    B.   Using technology to replace teachers in the classroom.
    C.   Ensuring that technology aligns with students' individual needs and enhances their learning experiences.
    D.   Focusing on technology that is easy to use for both teachers and students.

Answer:

QUESTION 87

Ms. Johnson is a special education teacher who is working with a diverse group of students in her inclusive classroom. She is implementing Response to Intervention (RTI) strategies to monitor student progress. She has observed that one of her students, Sarah, is struggling with reading comprehension and has not shown significant improvement despite receiving targeted interventions. Ms. Johnson decides to modify the assessment to gather more comprehensive data about Sarah's reading abilities. What is the most appropriate modification to the assessment to gather data about Sarah's reading comprehension?

    A.   Administer the same assessment but with fewer questions to reduce the testing time for Sarah.
    B.   Provide Sarah with an easier reading passage to increase her confidence during the assessment.
    C.   Use a different reading assessment that includes visual aids and graphic organizers.
    D.   Administer a higher-level reading comprehension test to challenge Sarah's abilities.

Answer:

QUESTION 88

Mr. Anderson, a special education teacher, is conducting an RTI assessment to identify areas where his student, Michael, is struggling in math. During the assessment, Mr. Anderson notices that Michael is becoming increasingly frustrated and anxious, which is affecting his performance. What should Mr. Anderson do to support Michael during the RTI assessment?

    A.   Encourage Michael to take a break and skip the challenging questions.
    B.   Provide additional time for Michael to complete the assessment.
    C.   Offer verbal praise and reassurance to help reduce Michael's anxiety.
    D.   Modify the assessment content to match Michael's instructional level.

Answer:

QUESTION 89

Ms. Ramirez is a special education teacher working with a group of students with various learning needs. She has implemented an RTI-based intervention to improve their writing skills. After a few weeks of intervention, she wants to assess their progress and identify if any student needs additional support. Which type of multi-level assessment is most appropriate for Ms. Ramirez to monitor her students' progress in writing?

A. A standardized writing test with set prompts for all students to ensure consistency.

B. An informal writing sample where students can choose their own writing topics.

C. An oral assessment where students explain their writing process and ideas.

D. A collaborative peer review session where students provide feedback to each other.

Answer:

QUESTION 90

Mr. Thomas is a special education teacher who is working with a student, John, who has attention difficulties. He wants to monitor John's progress in math and determine if the interventions provided are effective. What assessment modification should Mr. Thomas consider to accommodate John's attention difficulties during the RTI assessment?

A. Use a timer to ensure John completes the assessment within a specific timeframe.

B. Provide John with a quiet and separate testing environment to minimize distractions.

C. Administer the assessment in a group setting to encourage competition among students.

D. Break the assessment into smaller segments and allow John to take short breaks between sections.

Answer:

QUESTION 91

Ms. Lee is a special education teacher working with a group of students who have reading difficulties. She wants to identify their reading levels and design appropriate interventions to improve their skills. Which assessment strategy is most effective for Ms. Lee to determine her students' reading levels and provide targeted interventions?

A. Assign the students to read books independently and take comprehension quizzes afterward.

B. Use a reading level assessment tool that includes a variety of reading passages and questions.

C. Ask the students to write a summary of a book they have recently read.

D. Observe the students' performance during class reading activities and discussions.

Answer:

QUESTION 92

Ms. Jackson, a special education teacher, is part of a multidisciplinary team that is reviewing assessment data to determine a student's eligibility for special education services. The student, Alex, has been struggling academically, and the team is trying to make appropriate program and placement decisions. Which assessment information should Ms. Jackson prioritize when making eligibility and program decisions for Alex?

A. Standardized test scores from the most recent state assessment.

B. Teacher observations of Alex's behavior in the classroom.

C. Results from a cognitive assessment administered by a licensed psychologist.

D. Anecdotal notes from previous teachers about Alex's academic progress.

Answer:

QUESTION 93

Mr. Roberts, a special education teacher, is planning instruction for a student, Emily, who has specific learning disabilities in reading and writing. He wants to monitor Emily's progress and evaluate the effectiveness of his instructional strategies.Which type of assessment would be most suitable for Mr. Roberts to monitor Emily's progress and evaluate the effectiveness of his instruction

    A. A standardized reading and writing test provided to all students in the grade level.
    B. A teacher-designed quiz with questions based on the current lesson's content.
    C. A progress monitoring tool that assesses Emily's reading and writing skills at regular intervals.
    D. A group project where Emily collaborates with her classmates on a writing assignment.

Answer:

QUESTION 94

A team of special education teachers and therapists is collaborating to develop an Individualized Education Program (IEP) for a student named Liam, who has a physical disability and uses a wheelchair. They want to ensure that Liam's needs are met to support his learning and participation in the school environment. Which assessment information is crucial for the team to consider when planning Liam's IEP and making placement decisions?

    A. Liam's medical history and records related to his physical disability.
    B. Academic test scores from previous school years.
    C. Information about Liam's hobbies and extracurricular interests.
    D. Anecdotal reports from Liam's classmates about his social interactions.

Answer:

QUESTION 95

Ms. Chang is a special education teacher working with a diverse group of students with various learning needs. She wants to assess their understanding of a complex math concept. Which assessment strategy would be most effective for Ms. Chang to determine her students' comprehension of the complex math concept?

    A. Administer a multiple-choice test with questions of increasing difficulty.
    B. Assign a research project on real-life applications of the math concept.
    C. Conduct one-on-one interviews to discuss the math concept in-depth.
    D. Use a group discussion format to encourage students to explain the concept to each other.

Answer:

QUESTION 96

Mr. Rodriguez, a special education teacher, is working with a student, Maria, who has a speech and language disorder. He wants to develop appropriate goals and objectives for her Individualized Education Program (IEP). What type of assessment information should Mr. Rodriguez use to develop appropriate speech and language goals for Maria?

    A. Maria's performance on a standardized language assessment.
    B. Feedback from Maria's classmates about her communication skills.
    C. Observations of Maria's social interactions during recess and lunchtime.
    D. A self-assessment survey completed by Maria about her language abilities.

Answer:

QUESTION 97

Mrs. Smith, a special education teacher, notices that one of her students, Alex, is struggling with reading and writing skills. She wants to gather more information to determine if Alex needs further assessment for possible special education services. What is the most appropriate first step Mrs. Smith should take to address Alex's learning difficulties?

A. Refer Alex for a comprehensive psychoeducational assessment.

B. Conduct a formal pre-referral intervention with evidence-based strategies.

C. Administer a standardized reading and writing test to assess Alex's abilities.

D. Observe Alex in various classroom settings to gather behavioral data.

Answer:

QUESTION 98

Mr. Johnson, a special education coordinator, is reviewing referral documents for a student, Emily, who has been referred for possible special education services due to academic and behavioral concerns. What should Mr. Johnson consider first when reviewing Emily's referral documents?

A. The recommendations provided by Emily's previous teachers.

B. Emily's academic performance on standardized tests.

C. Information about the specific academic and behavioral concerns.

D. Emily's attendance and punctuality records.

Answer:

QUESTION 99

Ms. Ramirez, a special education teacher, is involved in the eligibility determination process for a student, John, who has been referred for special education services. The team has gathered assessment data and other relevant information about John's academic performance and behavior. What is the primary purpose of the eligibility determination process?

A. To identify John's specific learning strengths and weaknesses.

B. To determine whether John's parents are supportive of special education services.

C. To decide which classroom setting is most suitable for John's education.

D. To establish whether John meets the criteria for receiving special education services.

Answer:

QUESTION 100

Mr. Thompson, a special education coordinator, is conducting a screening process to identify students who may need additional support. During the screening, he reviews various data, including academic performance and behavior.
What is the main goal of the screening process?

A. To identify students who require individualized educational plans (IEPs).

B. To determine students' eligibility for grade retention.

C. To identify students who may need further assessment or intervention.

D. To evaluate the effectiveness of school-wide instructional practices.

Answer:

QUESTION 101

Ms. Davis, a special education teacher, is part of a multidisciplinary team reviewing a student's assessment data to make an eligibility decision for special education services. What is the appropriate role of Ms. Davis in the eligibility decision-making process?

A. To advocate for the student's inclusion in general education settings.
B. To provide emotional support to the student and their family during the process.
C. To contribute her expertise and insights about the student's learning needs.
D. To oversee the administration of standardized tests for the eligibility determination.

Answer:

QUESTION 102

Mr. Johnson, a special education teacher, is preparing to assess a student with a learning disability in reading comprehension. The student is non-verbal and communicates using a communication device. Which assessment strategy should Mr. Johnson use to assess the student's reading comprehension effectively?

A. Traditional paper-and-pencil reading comprehension test.
B. Allow the student to respond orally to questions.
C. Modify the reading material to match the student's interest and abilities.
D. Use the student's communication device to present questions and obtain responses.

Answer:

QUESTION 103

During a standardized assessment, a special education teacher notices that a student with attention deficit hyperactivity disorder (ADHD) is having difficulty staying focused and completing the tasks within the time limits. What procedure can the teacher implement to accommodate this student effectively?

A. Providing the student with extra time to complete the assessment.
B. Assigning a peer buddy to read the questions aloud to the student.
C. Reducing the number of questions in the assessment.
D. Allowing the student to take breaks as needed during the assessment.

Answer:

QUESTION 104

Which technology-based assessment tool can special education teachers use to promote more objective and unbiased assessments, particularly for students from diverse cultural backgrounds?

A. Audio recording the students' responses to review later.
B. Utilizing online, multiple-choice questionnaires.
C. Incorporating virtual reality simulations for performance assessments.
D. Using automatic language translation for written assessments.

Answer:

QUESTION 105

Ms. Hernandez is a special education teacher administering an assessment to a student with a physical disability that affects their fine motor skills. The assessment involves drawing diagrams and labeling them. What accommodation can Ms. Hernandez provide to ensure the student's fine motor difficulties do not interfere with their knowledge demonstration?

    A. Allowing the student to describe the diagrams orally instead of drawing them.
    B. Assigning a scribe to draw and label the diagrams as directed by the student.
    C. Providing the student with a pre-drawn template for labeling the diagrams.
    D. Exempting the student from the drawing and labeling portions of the assessment.

Answer:

QUESTION 106

The Evaluation Team Report (ETR) for a student with a specific learning disability has been completed, and the IEP team is convening to develop the Individualized Education Program (IEP). As a special education teacher, what is your role in this process?

    A. Lead the meeting and make all decisions regarding the IEP content.
    B. Provide input on the student's strengths, needs, and appropriate goals.
    C. Ensure that all general education teachers sign the IEP document.
    D. Review the student's test scores and determine eligibility for special education.

Answer:

QUESTION 107

When developing a transition plan for a student with a disability, what is the primary focus for the IEP team?

    A. Determining the student's eligibility for college or vocational training.
    B. Establishing the specific career path the student should pursue after graduation.
    C. Outlining a comprehensive plan to support the student's successful transition to adulthood.
    D. Reviewing the student's past academic performance and attendance records.

Answer:

QUESTION 108

As a special education teacher involved in developing a Behavioral Intervention Plan (BIP), what is your main objective?

    A. Implementing consequences for students' challenging behaviors.
    B. Utilizing a standardized BIP template for all students with behavior issues.
    C. Creating an individualized plan to address and modify specific challenging behaviors.
    D. Assigning detentions and suspensions for students displaying behavioral difficulties.

Answer:

QUESTION 109

The IEP team is reviewing the progress of a student with autism who has been receiving special education services for six months. The student's parents are concerned about their child's slow progress. What role do the parents/guardians play in the IEP review process?

  A. Making all decisions regarding the necessary modifications to the IEP.
  B. Participating as equal members of the IEP team and providing valuable input.
  C. Observing the classroom to assess the effectiveness of special education services.
  D. Creating an entirely new IEP for the student without input from the IEP team.

Answer:

QUESTION 110

What is the primary responsibility of general education teachers regarding the implementation of a student's IEP in the inclusive classroom?

  A. Provide the same instruction to all students regardless of their IEP goals.
  B. Collaborate with the special education teacher to develop the IEP goals.
  C. Modify the curriculum to match the student's IEP objectives and provide accommodations.
  D. Assess the student solely based on their grade-level academic standards.

Answer:

QUESTION 111

You are a special education teacher conducting an initial assessment for a student with suspected learning difficulties. During the assessment, the student shows significant challenges with reading, writing, and spelling. Which of the following steps should you take next?

  A. Recommend immediate placement in special education classes.
  B. Conduct further assessments to gather more comprehensive data.
  C. Request a meeting with the student's parents to discuss the results.
  D. Implement individualized accommodations without delay.

Answer:

QUESTION 112

When developing an Individualized Education Program (IEP) for a student with a disability, which of the following is the most appropriate order of steps?

  A. Set annual goals, develop accommodations, determine present levels, and identify related services.
  B. Determine present levels, identify related services, develop accommodations, and set annual goals.
  C. Identify related services, determine present levels, set annual goals, and develop accommodations.
  D. Determine present levels, set annual goals, develop accommodations, and identify related services.

Answer:

QUESTION 113

During the assessment process, why is it crucial for special education teachers to consider a student's cultural and linguistic background?

A. To determine the student's potential for academic success.
B. To ensure the assessment results are aligned with grade-level expectations.
C. To avoid any potential biases or misinterpretations of the student's abilities.
D. To identify the most appropriate accommodations for the student.

Answer:

QUESTION 114

Which of the following best describes the purpose of progress monitoring in the context of program planning for students with disabilities?

A. Assessing whether a student qualifies for special education services.
B. Evaluating the effectiveness of the instructional strategies.
C. Determining the student's learning style and preferences.
D. Identifying specific strengths and weaknesses in the curriculum.

Answer:

QUESTION 115

As a special education teacher, you have been collaborating with the general education teacher and other specialists to develop an inclusive program for a student with autism spectrum disorder (ASD). The student has made significant progress in communication and social skills but continues to struggle with transitions and sensory sensitivities. What should be the focus of the program planning to address these challenges effectively?

A. Implementing individualized academic interventions.
B. Providing sensory breaks and accommodations during transitions.
C. Enrolling the student in extracurricular social skills classes.
D. Incorporating technology-based learning tools in the curriculum.

Answer:

QUESTION 116

You are a special education teacher preparing to create an inclusive learning environment for students with disabilities in a mainstream classroom. One of your students has a visual impairment and requires accommodations. What would be the most appropriate strategy for modifying the learning environment for this student?

A. Providing printed handouts in large font size.
B. Using a text-to-speech software for auditory access to materials.
C. Assigning a peer buddy to read aloud all materials for the student.
D. Encouraging the student to sit closer to the board to see better.

Answer:

QUESTION 117

In a special education classroom, you have students with various learning disabilities, including dyslexia and dysgraphia. You want to create a structured and organized learning environment to support their needs. What is the best modification strategy to achieve this goal?

    A.   Allowing students to choose their learning activities freely.
    B.   Using a reward system for completing assignments on time.
    C.   Providing visual schedules and checklists for daily activities.
    D.   Encouraging peer tutoring for students with learning disabilities.

Answer:

QUESTION 118

You have a student with attention-deficit/hyperactivity disorder (ADHD) in your class. The student often gets distracted and has difficulty staying focused during lessons. What is the most appropriate strategy to manage the learning environment for this student?

    A.   Assigning extra homework to keep the student engaged at home.
    B.   Seating the student near the classroom window for better natural light.
    C.   Providing opportunities for movement and brain breaks during lessons.
    D.   Allowing the student to use electronic devices for entertainment during class.

Answer:

QUESTION 119

As a special education teacher, you are responsible for managing the learning environment for students with various disabilities. One of your students has a specific learning disability in mathematics and struggles with grasping mathematical concepts. What would be the best approach to modify the learning environment for this student?

    A.   Reducing the complexity of math problems and assignments.
    B.   Assigning advanced math problems to challenge the student.
    C.   Allowing the student to use a calculator for all math tasks.
    D.   Removing the student from math class to avoid frustration.

Answer:

QUESTION 120

You are a special education teacher working with a small group of students with diverse learning needs. One of the students has social anxiety and finds it challenging to participate actively in group discussions. What is the most effective method to foster this student's active participation in the small-group setting?

    A.   Encourage the student to take on a leadership role in the group.
    B.   Assign the student individual tasks instead of group activities.
    C.   Create a supportive and non-judgmental environment for sharing.
    D.   Use competitive activities to motivate the student to participate.

Answer:

QUESTION 121

As a special education teacher, you are responsible for facilitating the integration of a student with autism into a large-group classroom setting. The student tends to become overwhelmed during assemblies and other large-group activities. What strategy would be most beneficial in this situation?

    A. Providing the student with noise-canceling headphones during large-group activities.
    B. Allowing the student to skip large-group activities to reduce anxiety.
    C. Assigning a teacher's aide to accompany the student during large-group events.
    D. Conducting social skills training specifically for large-group interactions.

Answer:

QUESTION 122

You have a one-to-one session with a student who has a learning disability in reading. The student often becomes frustrated and discouraged when encountering difficult words. What is the best method to foster the student's individual academic success during reading sessions?

    A. Decrease the reading difficulty to avoid frustration.
    B. Provide constant corrections to improve reading accuracy.
    C. Incorporate multi-sensory techniques, such as phonics and sight words.
    D. Allow the student to choose non-reading activities during sessions.

Answer:

QUESTION 123

You are a special education teacher working in a diverse classroom with students from various cultural backgrounds. What is an effective method to facilitate students' integration and promote a sense of belonging in the classroom?

    A. Organizing a multicultural fair to celebrate different cultures.
    B. Grouping students based on their cultural similarities for projects.
    C. Discouraging students from discussing cultural differences to avoid conflicts.
    D. Implementing a color-blind approach to ignore cultural differences.

Answer:

QUESTION 124

You have a student with a specific learning disability in memory retention. The student struggles to remember information for tests and exams. What is the most effective method to teach this student learning strategies to compensate for their memory deficits?

    A. Providing pre-written study notes for all the lessons.
    B. Encouraging the student to rely on rote memorization techniques.
    C. Teaching mnemonic devices and memory aids for better recall.
    D. Reducing the amount of information covered in each lesson.

Answer:

QUESTION 125

You are working with a student who has attention deficit hyperactivity disorder (ADHD) and struggles with staying focused during independent study sessions. What is the most effective way to teach this student self-assessment strategies to improve their focus and academic performance?

A. Providing the student with external rewards for completing tasks.
B. Assigning shorter study sessions with frequent breaks.
C. Using a timer and encouraging the student to track their focus time.
D. Allowing the student to listen to music during study sessions.

Answer:

QUESTION 126

You have a student with a language processing disorder who often misunderstands written instructions and verbal information. What is the most effective method to teach this student cognitive strategies for better comprehension?

A. Simplifying all instructions and content to basic language.
B. Encouraging the student to rely on others for clarifications.
C. Teaching the student to identify keywords and context clues.
D. Allowing the student extra time to complete assignments.

Answer:

QUESTION 127

You have a student who frequently struggles with perception and visual processing. They find it challenging to follow the sequence of steps in complex tasks. What is the most effective method to teach this student learning strategies to compensate for their deficits in perception and sequencing.

A. Breaking complex tasks into smaller, manageable steps.
B. Providing the student with written transcripts of verbal instructions.
C. Using audio recordings for all instructions and class materials.
D. Assigning a peer buddy to assist the student during tasks.

Answer:

QUESTION 128

You have a student with autism who displays challenging behaviors in the classroom when presented with academic tasks that are difficult for them. The behaviors include hitting their desk and refusing to engage with the task. What is the most appropriate step to take first when conducting a functional behavior assessment (FBA) for this student?

A. Implementing a token economy system to reinforce positive behaviors.
B. Interviewing the student's parents to gather information about the behaviors.
C. Observing the student during academic tasks to identify triggers and consequences.
D. Conducting a review of the student's academic progress and performance.

Answer:

QUESTION 129

You are developing a behavioral intervention plan (BIP) for a student with a learning disability who frequently disrupts the class by talking out of turn and making inappropriate comments. What is a crucial component to include in the BIP?

    A. Implementing a punishment system to deter the disruptive behaviors.
    B. Providing the student with additional academic support during disruptions.
    C. Identifying replacement behaviors and teaching appropriate social skills.
    D. Removing the student from the classroom during disruptive episodes.

Answer:

QUESTION 130

You have a student with attention-deficit/hyperactivity disorder (ADHD) who struggles to stay on task during independent work. The student often daydreams and fails to complete assignments. What is an effective modification to make in the behavioral intervention plan (BIP) to support this student?

    A. Increasing the number of assignments to improve focus.
    B. Allowing the student to work in a quiet, isolated environment.
    C. Using a visual timer to break the work into manageable segments.
    D. Providing rewards only if the student completes all assignments.

Answer:

QUESTION 131

You are monitoring the effectiveness of a behavioral intervention plan (BIP) for a student with a communication disorder who exhibits disruptive behaviors when frustrated. What data should you collect to evaluate the success of the BIP?

    A. The student's performance on academic assessments.
    B. The frequency and intensity of the disruptive behaviors.
    C. Feedback from the student's peers and teachers.
    D. The student's attendance and punctuality at school.

Answer:

QUESTION 132

You have a student with a physical disability who uses a wheelchair and has limited mobility. The student is interested in pursuing a career in computer programming. What is the most effective career and vocational program to support this student's aspirations?

    A. Providing job shadowing opportunities in a computer programming company.
    B. Enrolling the student in a vocational training program for office administration.
    C. Arranging internships at local businesses with accessibility accommodations.
    D. Facilitating online coding courses tailored to the student's specific interests.

Answer:

QUESTION 133

As a special education teacher, you have a diverse classroom with students from various cultural and linguistic backgrounds. What is an effective strategy for developing instructional content that is responsive to these students' differences?

A. Using standardized textbooks and materials to maintain consistency.
B. Incorporating multicultural literature and diverse perspectives in lessons.
C. Focusing on one dominant cultural perspective to avoid confusion.
D. Assigning separate tasks for students based on their cultural backgrounds.

Answer:

QUESTION 134

You have a student with a specific learning disability in reading who is also an English language learner. What is the best approach to developing instructional content that addresses both the student's reading difficulties and language barriers?

A. Providing extra reading practice using grade-level English texts.
B. Using simplified reading materials to match the student's English proficiency.
C. Incorporating bilingual resources and translated materials.
D. Focusing solely on improving the student's reading skills in English.

Answer:

QUESTION 135

You are developing an effective transition program for students with disabilities to prepare them for post-school life. What is a crucial component to include in the program?

A. Providing students with lists of potential job opportunities.
B. Arranging visits to various college campuses for career exploration.
C. Facilitating vocational training exclusively for specific disabilities.
D. Offering opportunities for community-based work experiences.

Answer:

QUESTION 136

During a classroom discussion, a student with autism spectrum disorder (ASD) is showing signs of frustration, such as rocking back and forth and avoiding eye contact. The other students seem disinterested in the topic. As a special education teacher, what is the most effective strategy to address this situation and establish rapport with all students?

A. Ask the student with ASD to leave the classroom temporarily to calm down.
B. Redirect the classroom discussion to a topic that interests the other students.
C. Provide a visual schedule or agenda for the discussion and check in with the student with ASD privately afterward.
D. Allow the other students to continue their disinterested behavior, as they are not directly involved.

Answer:

QUESTION 137

As a special education teacher, you have a student with a specific learning disability who often becomes anxious during tests, leading to reduced performance. What is the most effective way to support this student and establish rapport with them?

A. Provide extra time and allow the student to take the test alone in a separate room.
B. Advise the student to take deep breaths and relax before the test.
C. Offer the student an alternative assessment method, such as an oral exam.
D. Help the student create a study group with peers to reduce anxiety.

Answer:

QUESTION 138

A new student with a hearing impairment has joined your inclusive classroom. What is the best way to establish rapport and create an inclusive environment for this student and their classmates?

A. Assign a sign language interpreter to the student and provide subtitles for all classroom videos.
B. Seat the student near the front of the classroom and provide written materials in large print.
C. Encourage other students to learn basic sign language to communicate with their new classmate.
D. Implement visual aids and demonstrations to supplement verbal instructions and explanations.

Answer:

QUESTION 139

In your inclusive classroom, a student with attention-deficit/hyperactivity disorder (ADHD) frequently interrupts your lessons and blurts out answers without raising their hand. Other students have started to complain about the disruptions. How can you address this situation and maintain rapport with the entire class?

A. Speak to the student privately and ask them to control their impulses during lessons.
B. Assign the student with ADHD additional homework as a consequence of their disruptive behavior.
C. Implement a hand-raising rule for all students and acknowledge and redirect positive behaviors.
D. Isolate the student with ADHD in a designated area during lessons to avoid disruptions.

Answer:

QUESTION 140

In your special education classroom, a student with emotional and behavioral disorders frequently becomes agitated and aggressive towards other students when faced with challenging tasks. What is the most effective strategy to modify the learning environment and manage this behavior?

A. Remove all challenging tasks from the student's curriculum to prevent agitation.
B. Implement a behavior intervention plan with positive reinforcement for appropriate behaviors.
C. Isolate the student in a separate room whenever they show signs of agitation.
D. Allow the student to leave the classroom whenever they feel overwhelmed.

Answer:

QUESTION 141

As a special education teacher, you have a student with autism spectrum disorder (ASD) who experiences sensory overload during classroom activities, leading to disruptive behaviors. What is the best strategy to modify the learning environment and prevent sensory overload?

A. Reduce all classroom activities to minimize sensory stimuli.
B. Provide the student with noise-canceling headphones and a quiet corner for breaks.
C. Remove the student from the classroom whenever sensory overload occurs.
D. Assign a teacher's aide solely dedicated to the student's sensory needs.

Answer:

QUESTION 142

In your special education classroom, a student with a specific learning disability becomes increasingly frustrated when working on math assignments, often leading to emotional outbursts. What is the most appropriate crisis prevention strategy to employ in this situation?

A. Assign more challenging math assignments to improve the student's skills gradually.
B. Allow the student to skip math assignments when they feel overwhelmed.
C. Implement a gradual desensitization plan to math tasks and provide emotional support.
D. Remove math assignments from the student's curriculum entirely to prevent emotional outbursts.

Answer:

QUESTION 143

As a special education teacher, you have a student with attention-deficit/hyperactivity disorder (ADHD) who frequently exhibits impulsive behaviors during group activities, leading to conflicts with peers. What is the best strategy to modify the learning environment and manage these impulsive behaviors effectively?

A. Exclude the student from all group activities to prevent conflicts.
B. Provide the student with an individualized reward system for staying focused.
C. Assign a teacher's aide to monitor and intervene in group activities.
D. Implement clear rules and visual cues for turn-taking during group activities.

Answer:

QUESTION 144

In your inclusive classroom, you have a student with a specific learning disability who struggles with reading comprehension. They often have difficulty understanding complex texts and connecting ideas. What is the most effective strategy to help this student recognize relationships across disciplines and improve reading comprehension?

A. Provide the student with simplified texts that focus solely on the main ideas.
B. Encourage the student to listen to audio recordings of the complex texts.
C. Use graphic organizers and concept maps to visually represent relationships and connections in the texts.
D. Assign extra reading assignments to the student to practice comprehension.

Answer:

QUESTION 145

As a special education teacher, you have a student with autism spectrum disorder (ASD) who has a keen interest in science but struggles with understanding abstract concepts. How can you facilitate maintenance and generalization of academic skills for this student?

A. Assign the student additional science homework to reinforce abstract concepts.
B. Provide the student with hands-on science experiments to make abstract concepts tangible.
C. Encourage the student to focus solely on their area of interest to avoid confusion.
D. Reduce the complexity of science topics to match the student's cognitive level.

Answer:

QUESTION 146

In your diverse classroom, you have students with varying language proficiency levels, including English language learners (ELLs). What is an effective strategy to teach essential vocabulary and content across the general curriculum while accommodating the needs of ELLs?

A. Provide ELLs with separate language instruction and exclude them from content-based lessons.
B. Simplify the curriculum to match the language proficiency level of ELLs.
C. Use visual aids, realia, and context-rich examples to make content more accessible to ELLs.
D. Assign ELLs to peer tutors to improve their language skills.

Answer:

QUESTION 147

As a special education teacher, you have students with various cognitive abilities and learning styles in your classroom. What is an effective strategy to help students recognize relationships across disciplines and promote interdisciplinary learning?

A. Keep subjects separated and avoid integrating content from different disciplines.
B. Use only traditional teaching methods and avoid experiential learning activities.
C. Encourage students to explore connections between different subjects through projects and real-life applications.
D. Assign students to study groups based on their cognitive abilities.

Answer:

QUESTION 148

In your inclusive classroom, two students with autism spectrum disorder (ASD) frequently engage in conflicts during group activities. They struggle to resolve disagreements and often become frustrated with each other. What is the most effective strategy to teach problem-solving and conflict-resolution skills to these students?

A. Assign the students to different groups to avoid conflicts.
B. Provide the students with a written conflict-resolution guide to follow.
C. Facilitate role-playing exercises to model and practice problem-solving strategies.
D. Allow the students to work independently to minimize opportunities for conflicts.

Answer:

QUESTION 149

As a special education teacher, you have a student with emotional and behavioral disorders who often reacts impulsively and aggressively to frustrating situations. What is an effective strategy to teach the student appropriate expectations for personal and social behavior?

    A. Isolate the student from social settings to prevent aggressive reactions.
    B. Use a behavior chart to publicly display the student's problematic behaviors.
    C. Develop a behavior plan that explicitly outlines expected behaviors and positive reinforcement for compliance.
    D. Allow the student to self-monitor their behavior without external interventions.

Answer:

QUESTION 150

In your special education classroom, you have students with various learning disabilities and attention issues. They often struggle to work cooperatively during group projects, leading to unproductive and disorganized outcomes. What is the most effective strategy to teach problem-solving and cooperation skills to these students?

    A. Assign individual projects to each student to avoid collaboration challenges.
    B. Divide the students into groups randomly to foster new social connections.
    C. Provide structured group activities with defined roles and expectations.
    D. Eliminate group projects and focus solely on individual tasks.

Answer:

QUESTION 151

As a special education teacher, you have a student who often experiences sensory overload in busy environments, leading to meltdowns and conflicts with peers. What is an effective strategy to teach this student self-regulation and conflict-resolution skills in overwhelming situations?

    A. Provide the student with a sensory break area where they can go to calm down.
    B. Remove the student from all busy environments to prevent sensory overload.
    C. Assign a peer buddy to intervene during the student's meltdowns.
    D. Use a behavior chart to track the student's conflicts with peers.

Answer:

QUESTION 152

You have a student with autism spectrum disorder (ASD) who will be transitioning from high school to postsecondary education. The student has expressed concerns about the new environment and changes in routine. What is the most effective strategy to promote a successful transition for this student?

    A. Provide the student with a detailed schedule of their new postsecondary education routine.
    B. Arrange for the student to visit the postsecondary education facility before the transition.
    C. Advise the student to avoid thinking about the upcoming changes to reduce anxiety.
    D. Assign a peer mentor from the postsecondary institution to support the student.

Answer:

QUESTION 153

As a special education teacher, you have a student with a learning disability who will be transitioning from one grade level to another within the same school. The student is worried about coping with new academic expectations. What is the most effective strategy to promote a successful transition for this student?

A. Introduce the student to the new teachers and classmates a week before the transition.
B. Provide the student with the curriculum for the upcoming grade level to review in advance.
C. Assign the student additional homework to prepare for the higher academic expectations.
D. Hold a meeting with the student's parents to discuss strategies for managing the transition.

Answer:

QUESTION 154

You have a student with intellectual disabilities who will be transitioning from high school to adulthood and entering the workforce. The student is eager but uncertain about the job search process. What is the most effective strategy to promote a successful transition to employment for this student?

A. Assist the student in creating a comprehensive resume highlighting their strengths and skills.
B. Arrange for the student to have a trial work experience in various job settings.
C. Encourage the student to explore postsecondary education opportunities instead of immediate employment.
D. Provide the student with a list of potential job openings and contact information.

Answer:

QUESTION 155

As a special education teacher, you have a student with attention-deficit/hyperactivity disorder (ADHD) who will be transitioning from elementary school to middle school. The student is concerned about managing multiple classrooms and assignments. What is the most effective strategy to promote a successful transition for this student?

A. Provide the student with detailed organizational tools and time management resources.
B. Arrange for the student to have an individualized aide to support them during the transition.
C. Assign the student to a single classroom with specialized instruction to ease the transition.
D. Encourage the student to rely on their memory and instincts to manage assignments.

Answer:

QUESTION 156

You have a student with ADHD in your special education classroom who often struggles to maintain attention during class activities. What is the most effective strategy to help maintain the student's attention?

A. Implementing a reward system where the student earns points for staying focused.
B. Allowing the student to take frequent breaks during class to reduce restlessness.
C. Assigning the student additional homework to reinforce learning outside of class.
D. Using visual aids and hands-on activities to make the lessons more engaging.

Answer:

QUESTION 157

When establishing behavioral expectations for students with disabilities in your classroom, what is the most important aspect to consider?

    A.   Setting consequences for inappropriate behavior.
    B.   Comparing the students' behavior with their peers.
    C.   Tailoring the expectations to each student's individual needs.
    D.   Enforcing strict rules and regulations to maintain discipline.

Answer:

QUESTION 158

A new student with autism spectrum disorder (ASD) has joined your class. They are sensitive to changes in routines and may experience anxiety when the schedule is disrupted. What is the best strategy for supporting this student's need for a consistent daily routine?

    A.   Introducing surprising elements during the day to help the student adapt to changes better.
    B.   Sticking strictly to the routine, avoiding any modifications or adjustments.
    C.   Gradually introducing changes in the routine while providing advance notice and visual schedules.
    D.   Assigning a peer buddy to the student to help them cope with any changes in the routine.

Answer:

QUESTION 159

In promoting independence among students with disabilities, which strategy is most effective for encouraging them to take more responsibility for their learning?

    A.   Assigning a teaching assistant to provide constant support and guidance.
    B.   Allowing the students to skip difficult tasks to avoid frustration.
    C.   Breaking tasks into manageable steps and offering positive reinforcement for completion.
    D.   Providing detailed and explicit instructions for every activity.

Answer:

QUESTION 160

In your inclusive classroom, you have a student with dyslexia who struggles with reading comprehension. What is the most effective instructional practice to promote this student's success in the general curriculum

    A.   Providing the student with alternative assignments to avoid reading-heavy tasks.
    B.   Using audiobooks for all reading materials to accommodate the student's needs.
    C.   Implementing multi-sensory approaches to reading instruction, such as Orton-Gillingham.
    D.   Assigning a peer tutor to read aloud to the student during class.

Answer:

QUESTION 161

When differentiating instruction for students with varying abilities in a general education classroom, what is the most important consideration?

A. Providing gifted students with more challenging assignments to keep them engaged.
B. Focusing on the students' weaknesses to help them catch up with their peers.
C. Adapting instruction to meet the individual needs and learning styles of all students.
D. Assigning extra support staff to work with struggling students outside of the classroom.

Answer:

QUESTION 162

You have a student with attention deficit hyperactivity disorder (ADHD) who often becomes distracted during class lectures. What is the most effective instructional practice to promote this student's success in the general curium?

A. Providing the student with additional breaks to release pent-up energy and improve focus.
B. Allowing the student to use electronic devices during lectures for note-taking.
C. Providing the student with written summaries of the lecture content after each class.
D. Incorporating active learning strategies and frequent interactive discussions during lectures.

Answer:

QUESTION 163

In promoting students' success in the general curriculum, how can the use of technology be most effectively implemented?

A. Introducing technology as a reward for completing assignments to motivate students.
B. Using technology as a replacement for traditional teaching methods to modernize the classroom.
C. Incorporating technology that aligns with instructional goals and enhances student learning.
D. Assigning students to complete all their coursework exclusively on digital platforms.

Answer:

QUESTION 164

When working with students who have different cultural backgrounds and experiences in the general curriculum, what is the best approach for a teacher to take?

A. Focusing solely on teaching mainstream cultural values to promote assimilation.
B. Ignoring cultural differences to avoid potential misunderstandings.
C. Incorporating diverse perspectives and experiences into the curriculum.
D. Encouraging students to conform to the dominant cultural norms of the classroom.

Answer:

QUESTION 165

In your special education classroom, you have a student with autism who struggles with communication and social skills. What is the most effective strategy to help develop the student's communication abilities?

    A. Encouraging the use of gestures and sign language as the primary means of communication.
    B. Implementing a picture exchange communication system (PECS) to facilitate communication.
    C. Discouraging verbal communication to reduce frustration and promote alternative methods.
    D. Providing scripted phrases for the student to memorize and use during interactions.

Answer:

QUESTION 166

When providing behavioral interventions for students with disabilities, what is the most important aspect to consider?

    A. Applying the same intervention strategy for all students to maintain consistency.
    B. Using punishment-based methods to discourage undesirable behaviors.
    C. Conducting a functional behavior assessment to understand the reasons behind the behavior.
    D. Rewarding students only for academic achievements, not for behavioral improvements.

Answer:

QUESTION 167

In your special education classroom, you have a student with attention deficit hyperactivity disorder (ADHD) who frequently disrupts the class by blurting out answers and interrupting others. What is the most effective behavioral intervention to address this behavior?

    A. Applying a behavior contract that rewards the student for refraining from interrupting for a specific period.
    B. Using a behavior chart that publicly displays the student's interruptions to create awareness.
    C. Ignoring the interruptions to avoid reinforcing the behavior with attention.
    D. Implementing a daily time-out punishment for each interruption to deter future disruptions.

Answer:

QUESTION 168

What is the most effective strategy for promoting social skills development among students with disabilities?

    A. Organizing social skills training in large groups to expose students to a variety of peers.
    B. Encouraging solitary play to avoid potential social conflicts and misunderstandings.
    C. Implementing social narratives and role-playing activities to practice social interactions.
    D. Discouraging peer interactions to minimize distractions and focus on academic tasks.

Answer:

QUESTION 169

When teaching communication and social skills to students with disabilities, what is the best approach for ensuring generalization of these skills beyond the classroom?

    A. Limiting social interactions to controlled settings within the school environment.
    B. Encouraging students to only interact with other students who have similar disabilities.
    C. Collaborating with parents and caregivers to reinforce skills in various settings.
    D. Avoiding community outings and extracurricular activities to prevent overstimulation.

Answer:

QUESTION 170

You have a student with intellectual disabilities who will soon transition from high school to adulthood. WHat is the most effective strategy to promote a successful transition for this student?

A. Encouraging the student to pursue higher education at a traditional college or university.
B. Focusing solely on academic achievements to prepare the student for future career opportunities.
C. Implementing a transition plan that includes vocational training and community-based experiences.
D. Assigning the student to participate in extracurricular activities to build social skills.

Answer:

QUESTION 171

When teaching functional living skills to students with disabilities, what is the most effective approach?

A. Relying on rote memorization and repetitive drills to reinforce the skills.
B. Teaching skills in isolation without considering their relevance to daily life.
C. Utilizing real-life scenarios and incorporating the skills into meaningful activities.
D. Assigning worksheets and written exercises to assess the students' understanding.

Answer:

QUESTION 172

You have a student with autism who struggles with daily living skills, such as personal hygiene and self-care. What is the most effective way to support this student's development in these areas?

A. Completing the tasks for the student to ensure they are done correctly.
B. Providing visual schedules and step-by-step instructions for each task.
C. Setting consequences for incomplete or poorly performed tasks.
D. Assigning a peer mentor to assist the student with daily living skills.

Answer:

QUESTION 173

When preparing students with disabilities for the transition to post-secondary education or employment, what is the most important factor to consider?

A. Discouraging students from exploring their interests to focus on practical skills.
B. Exclusively emphasizing academic achievements to meet admission requirements.
C. Identifying and building on each student's strengths and talents.
D. Encouraging students to rely solely on support services in their new environment.

Answer:

QUESTION 174

What is the most effective way to facilitate successful community integration for students with disabilities?

A. Shielding students from community experiences to prevent potential challenges.
B. Promoting segregation in community settings to ensure their safety.
C. Providing opportunities for students to actively participate in community activities.
D. Relying solely on support staff to accompany students in community outings.

Answer:

QUESTION 175

Mrs. Johnson, a special education teacher, has a diverse group of students in her classroom, including students from different cultural backgrounds and varying abilities. She wants to create a safe and supportive classroom climate that fosters respect for diversity and positive interactions among all students. Which of the following strategies would be most effective for Mrs. Johnson to achieve her goal?

A. Implement a strict set of rules and consequences to maintain order and discipline in the classroom.
B. Allow students to form their own cliques and groups during class activities to encourage socialization.
C. Designate a specific area in the classroom for students to express their cultural identity through decorations and artwork.
D. Plan cooperative learning activities that require students to work together in diverse groups, promoting teamwork and understanding.

Answer:

QUESTION 176

Mr. Smith is a special education teacher with a class of students with various reading disabilities. He wants to provide effective reading instruction to all his students. Which research-supported method would be most appropriate for Mr. Smith to use in his classroom?

A. Whole Language Approach: Emphasizing the meaning and context of texts, encouraging students to guess words based on context.
B. Phonics Instruction: Teaching students to decode words by understanding the relationships between letters and sounds.
C. Sight Word Memorization: Having students memorize frequently used words to improve reading fluency.
D. Reciprocal Teaching: Encouraging students to take turns leading discussions about the content they read.

Answer:

QUESTION 177

Ms. Lee is a special education teacher with a diverse classroom that includes students with disabilities, various cultural and linguistic backgrounds, and some who use alternative and augmentative communication systems. She wants to foster their communication skills effectively. Which instructional strategy would be most appropriate for Ms. Lee to implement?

A. Using only verbal instructions and explanations to ensure consistency in communication across all students.
B. Implementing a rigid communication system for all students to follow, emphasizing uniformity.
C. Incorporating visual supports, such as picture cards and communication boards, to enhance understanding and expression.
D. Encouraging students to communicate primarily through their preferred mode, even if it hinders classroom cohesion.

Answer:

QUESTION 178

Mr. Davis is a special education teacher working with a group of high school students with diverse abilities. He wants to teach them essential daily living skills. Which teaching strategy would be most effective for Mr. Davis to use in this context?

A. Providing written instructions and worksheets for students to complete independently.
B. Demonstrating daily living tasks step-by-step and allowing students to practice under supervision.
C. Assigning online modules for students to learn daily living skills at their own pace.
D. Grouping students by ability and assigning specific tasks to each group for collaborative learning.

Answer:

QUESTION 179

A special education student with physical disabilities is joining a mainstream classroom. The student uses a wheelchair for mobility. The classroom has desks arranged in rows, making it difficult for the student to move around the room easily. What adaptation can the teacher make to the physical environment to provide optimal learning opportunities for the student with disabilities?

    A. Install a ramp at the classroom entrance.
    B. Rearrange the desks to create a U-shaped seating arrangement.
    C. Provide the student with a separate study area outside the classroom.
    D. Assign a peer buddy to assist the student in moving around the classroom.

Answer:

QUESTION 180

A special education teacher is working with a student with autism who has sensory sensitivities. The classroom is often too bright and noisy, leading to increased anxiety and difficulty concentrating for the student. Which adaptation can the teacher make to the physical environment to provide optimal learning opportunities for the student with autism?

    A. Install brighter lights to improve visibility.
    B. Play calming background music during class.
    C. Implement a sensory break area with dimmed lighting and noise-cancelling headphones.
    D. Assign a classroom aide to shadow the student and provide constant support.

Answer:

QUESTION 181

A special education teacher is working with a student who has a visual impairment. The student has difficulty accessing information presented on the standard classroom whiteboard.

What adaptation can the teacher make to the physical environment to provide optimal learning opportunities for the studentwith visual impairment?

    A. Provide the student with a magnifying glass to read the whiteboard.
    B. Use a larger font when writing on the whiteboard.
    C. Utilize an audio recording to convey the information on the whiteboard.
    D. Implement a digital whiteboard with screen-reader compatibility.

Answer:

QUESTION 182

A special education teacher is working with a student with dyslexia, and the student finds it challenging to read printed text in textbooks and handouts.

What adaptation can the teacher make to the physical environment to provide optimal learning opportunities for the student with dyslexia?

    A. Provide the student with a text-to-speech software to read the materials aloud.
    B. Assign a peer tutor to read the materials to the student.
    C. Use a different font style in handouts and textbooks to improve readability.
    D. Provide the student with larger textbooks with simplified language.

Answer:

QUESTION 183

A special education teacher is working with a student who has attention deficit hyperactivity disorder (ADHD). The student finds it challenging to stay focused and engaged during longer classroom activities. What adaptation can the teacher make to the physical environment to provide optimal learning opportunities for the student with ADHD?

    A. Increase the duration of classroom activities gradually to build the student's attention span.
    B. Provide the student with additional breaks during longer classroom activities.
    C. Seat the student near the front of the classroom to minimize distractions.
    D. Assign the student to lead group activities to encourage active participation.

Answer:

QUESTION 184

A special education teacher is working with a student with dyscalculia, a specific learning disability in mathematics. The student struggles with understanding and remembering math concepts and has difficulty recognizing numerical patterns. Which research-supported method is most effective for providing mathematics instruction to the student with dyscalculia?

    A. Implementing timed quizzes to encourage faster calculations.
    B. Providing hands-on manipulatives to explore math concepts visually and kinesthetically.
    C. Assigning advanced math problems to challenge the student's abilities.
    D. Using complex mathematical language to enhance the student's vocabulary.

Answer:

QUESTION 185

A special education teacher is working with a student with attention deficit hyperactivity disorder (ADHD). The student often becomes restless during math lessons and has difficulty staying on task. Which research-supported method can help the student with ADHD stay focused during math instruction?

    A. Providing breaks during math lessons to allow the student to release excess energy.
    B. Assigning the student extra math problems to keep them engaged.
    C. Using abstract visuals and diagrams to challenge the student's thinking.
    D. Encouraging the student to engage in parallel activities while listening to math lessons.

Answer:

QUESTION 186

A special education teacher is working with a student with a visual impairment. The student struggles with accessing information from standard printed math textbooks. Which research-supported method is the most effective for providing math instruction to the student with a visual impairment?

    A. Using audio recordings for all math materials.
    B. Providing the student with a sighted guide to explain visual information.
    C. Using tactile graphics and braille materials for math concepts.
    D. Increasing the font size in the printed math textbooks.

Answer:

QUESTION 187

A special education teacher is working with a student who has a learning disability in mathematics. The student has difficulty understanding abstract math concepts and often becomes frustrated during problem-solving tasks. Which research-supported method can help the student with learning disabilities in mathematics comprehend abstract concepts?

    A. Reducing the number of math assignments to alleviate frustration.
    B. Using real-life examples to relate abstract math concepts to practical situations.
    C. Providing memorization techniques for complex formulas and procedures.
    D. Encouraging competition among students to motivate the student to perform better.

Answer:

QUESTION 188

A special education teacher is working with a student who has an intellectual disability. The student has difficulty grasping basic number concepts and struggles with counting and sequencing numbers. Which research-supported method can help the student with an intellectual disability develop basic number sense?

    A. Engaging the student in complex mathematical problem-solving tasks.
    B. Using songs and rhymes to teach counting and number sequencing.
    C. Providing the student with pre-written solutions for math exercises.
    D. Assigning additional homework to practice number skills.

Answer:

QUESTION 189

A special education teacher is working with a student who has emotional and behavioral challenges. The student often struggles with managing anger and conflicts with peers, which affects their social interactions.

Which strategy is most effective for fostering the student's social skills and self-management?

    A. Isolating the student during conflicts to prevent disruptions.
    B. Implementing a behavior chart with public rewards for improved behavior.
    C. Teaching the student emotional regulation techniques and conflict resolution skills.
    D. Assigning the student a peer mentor to handle social situations on their behalf.

Answer:

QUESTION 190

A special education teacher is working with a high school student with a learning disability. The student often doubts their abilities and feels discouraged about their academic performance compared to their peers. Which strategy is most effective for increasing the student's self-esteem and self-awareness?

    A. Offering constant praise and rewards for completing tasks.
    B. Providing accommodations to ease the student's academic workload.
    C. Encouraging the student to set achievable goals and celebrate progress.
    D. Assigning the student to a remedial class for additional academic support.

Answer:

QUESTION 191

A special education teacher is working with a middle school student with autism. The student is capable of completing tasks independently but often struggles to express their needs or ask for help when necessary. Which strategy is most effective for developing self-advocacy skills in the student with autism?

    A. Assigning a teacher's aide to anticipate the student's needs and provide assistance.
    B. Implementing a visual schedule and communication cards to aid in expressing needs.
    C. Limiting the student's responsibilities to prevent overwhelming situations.
    D. Encouraging the student's peers to speak on their behalf during group activities.

Answer:

QUESTION 192

A special education teacher is working with a group of students with various disabilities. The students have shown increased interest in extracurricular activities but feel uncertain about joining due to their disabilities. Which strategy is most effective for fostering self-determination in the students with disabilities?

    A. Exempting the students from extracurricular activities to prevent potential disappointment.
    B. Organizing disability-specific extracurricular groups to ensure a supportive environment.
    C. Holding meetings with parents to discuss the potential challenges of joining activities.
    D. Providing information about inclusive extracurricular opportunities and offering support.

Answer:

QUESTION 193

A special education teacher is working with a student who has a physical disability. The student often faces barriers in accessing the school environment and has expressed concerns about limited participation in school decision-making. Which strategy is most effective for fostering self-advocacy and self-determination in the student with a physical disability?

    A. Assigning a personal aide to accompany the student during school hours.
    B. Advocating for accessibility modifications to the school environment.
    C. Discouraging the student from participating in school decision-making to reduce stress.
    D. Conducting regular meetings with the student to discuss their goals and concerns.

Answer:

QUESTION 194

A special education teacher is working with a group of high school students with diverse disabilities. The students have expressed an interest in exploring potential careers and vocational opportunities. Which strategy is most effective for promoting vocational/career competence in the students with disabilities?

    A. Providing the students with vocational assessments to identify suitable career options.
    B. Assigning the students to volunteer at local businesses to gain work experience.
    C. Focusing solely on academic subjects to prepare the students for future careers.
    D. Encouraging the students to attend workshops and career fairs to explore different industries.

Answer:

QUESTION 195

A special education teacher is working with a young adult with intellectual disabilities who is transitioning from school to post-school life. The student has expressed an interest in participating in leisure and recreational activities in the community. Which strategy is most effective for promoting the student's participation in community leisure and recreational activities?

    A. Organizing a special leisure program exclusively for individuals with disabilities.
    B. Collaborating with community organizations to provide inclusive recreational opportunities.
    C. Discouraging the student from participating in leisure activities to prevent potential challenges.
    D. Providing the student with leisure activities within the school setting.

Answer:

QUESTION 196

A special education teacher is working with a student with physical disabilities who aspires to pursue a career in technology. The student faces challenges in accessing technology and requires accommodations for computer use. Which strategy is most effective for teaching technology skills to promote the student's vocational competence?

    A. Providing the student with a specialized computer lab with assistive technology.
    B. Exempting the student from technology-related tasks to reduce frustration.
    C. Offering online tutorials and resources for the student to learn at their own pace.
    D. Encouraging the student to pursue a different vocational interest to avoid technology challenges.

Answer:

QUESTION 197

A special education teacher is working with a group of students with autism who are interested in developing vocational skills. The students have excellent memory and attention to detail but struggle with social interactions and communication. Which strategy is most effective for teaching vocational skills to the students with autism?

    A. Assigning group projects to encourage social interaction among the students.
    B. Providing written instructions and visual aids to support task completion.
    C. Exclusively focusing on vocational skills and neglecting social communication training.
    D. Assigning a vocational coach to communicate with potential employers on the students' behalf.

Answer:

QUESTION 198

A special education teacher is working with a student with a learning disability who is passionate about environmental conservation. The student wishes to explore potential career paths in this field. Which strategy is most effective for promoting the student's vocational competence in environmental conservation?

    A. Discouraging the student from pursuing a career in environmental conservation due to their learning disability.
    B. Providing the student with internship opportunities at local environmental organizations.
    C. Limiting the student's involvement to theoretical learning about environmental issues.
    D. Assigning the student tasks unrelated to environmental conservation to avoid potential challenges.

Answer:

QUESTION 199

Which federal law, enacted in 1975, mandated a free appropriate public education (FAPE) for all students with disabilities and ensured the provision of special education services in the least restrictive environment (LRE)?

A. Section 504 of the Rehabilitation Act
B. No Child Left Behind Act (NCLB)
C. Individuals with Disabilities Education Act (IDEA)
D. Elementary and Secondary Education Act (ESEA)

Answer:

QUESTION 200

Ms. Johnson, a special education teacher, is preparing an Individualized Education Program (IEP) for Tim, a 14-year-old student with autism. Tim has difficulty with social interactions and frequently engages in repetitive behaviors. Ms. Johnson wants to address these challenges in his IEP effectively. What would be the most appropriate goal for Tim's IEP?

A. Tim will improve his academic performance in all subjects by one grade level.
B. Tim will reduce repetitive behaviors by 50% within six months.
C. Tim will participate in at least one extracurricular activity to enhance social skills.
D. Tim will complete all homework assignments independently.

Answer:

QUESTION 201

Which court case led to the landmark decision affirming that students with disabilities have the right to a free appropriate public education (FAPE) in the least restrictive environment (LRE)?

A. Brown v. Board of Education
B. Mills v. Board of Education of the District of Columbia
C. Obergefell v. Hodges
D. New Jersey v. T.L.O.

Answer:

QUESTION 202

Which ethical principle guides special education teachers to prioritize the best interests of the students with disabilities they serve?

A. Justice
B. Autonomy
C. Fidelity
D. Beneficence

Answer:

QUESTION 203

Mr. Rodriguez, a special education teacher, is conducting an annual review meeting for a student with a specific learning disability. The student has made significant progress over the year and has achieved most of the goals set in the Individualized Education Program (IEP). However, the student continues to struggle with reading comprehension. What should Mr. Rodriguez consider during the annual review meeting?

   A. Recommending the student for a full inclusion program without special education support.
   B. Maintaining the current IEP goals as they are, as the student has shown progress.
   C. Developing new IEP goals focusing solely on reading comprehension improvement.
   D. Requesting a reevaluation to determine if the student's disability category needs to be changed.

Answer:

QUESTION 204

As a special education teacher, you are working with a general education teacher to support a student with a learning disability in their inclusive classroom. The general education teacher is unsure how to accommodate the student effectively.

What is the most appropriate strategy for collaborating with the general education teacher?

   A. Provide the general education teacher with a list of accommodations and modifications without discussing the student's specific needs.
   B. Schedule regular meetings to review the student's progress and discuss any concerns or adjustments needed.
   C. Take over the teaching responsibilities for the student with a learning disability to ensure their needs are met.
   D. Advise the general education teacher to lower the academic expectations for the student to reduce stress.

Answer:

QUESTION 205

Which of the following strategies is most effective for communicating with related services providers and other school staff members about the specific needs of a student with multiple disabilities?

   A. Sending generic emails with basic information about the student's disabilities.
   B. Holding a single meeting at the beginning of the school year to discuss all students with disabilities.
   C. Utilizing a secure online platform to share detailed information and progress updates regularly.
   D. Leaving notes in the student's backpack to inform related services providers about their needs.

Answer:

QUESTION 206

As a special education teacher, you have several teaching aides and paraprofessionals supporting students with disabilities in your classroom. You want to ensure effective supervision and collaboration. What is the best approach for working with teaching aides and paraprofessionals?

   A. Assigning fixed tasks and responsibilities to each aide, without providing opportunities for feedback or professional growth.
   B. Conducting regular team meetings to share information, discuss strategies, and provide opportunities for professional development.
   C. Minimizing communication with aides to maintain a clear distinction between your role as the teacher and their role as support staff.
   D. Relying solely on aides for instructional decisions and classroom management to alleviate your workload.

Answer:

QUESTION 207

Which approach is most effective for collaborating with representatives of community agencies to provide learning opportunities for students with disabilities after graduation?

    A. Requesting community agencies to take complete responsibility for creating learning opportunities independently.
    B. Engaging community agencies in a one-time meeting to discuss their available resources.
    C. Establishing ongoing partnerships with community agencies to develop personalized transition plans for each student.
    D. Contacting community agencies only when a student with disabilities expresses interest in a specific program.

Answer:

QUESTION 208

Ms. Martinez, a special education teacher, is working with a student who has difficulty with self-regulation and managing emotions. The student often becomes frustrated and has outbursts during challenging tasks.

What is the most effective strategy for Ms. Martinez to use when consulting with other school staff members to support the student?

    A. Advise staff members to ignore the student's outbursts and continue with their tasks.
    B. Discuss the student's challenges and progress in a single meeting at the end of the school year.
    C. Collaborate with staff members to develop a consistent behavior management plan and share regular progress updates.
    D. Inform staff members that the student's emotional regulation difficulties are temporary and will resolve on their own.

Answer:

QUESTION 209

Ms. Johnson, a special education teacher, is concerned about the overrepresentation of students from culturally diverse backgrounds in programs for students with disabilities. She wants to address this issue effectively. Which approach is most appropriate for her to take?

    A. Implementing a blanket referral process for all students showing academic challenges.
    B. Conducting individualized assessments and considering cultural and linguistic factors.
    C. Promoting inclusive education by mainstreaming all students in general education classrooms.
    D. Collaborating with other special education teachers to segregate students with disabilities.

Answer:

QUESTION 210

Which of the following historical events had a significant impact on shaping the field of special education?

    A. The invention of the printing press.
    B. The ratification of the Universal Declaration of Human Rights.
    C. The establishment of public education in the United States.
    D. The passing of the Civil Rights Act of 1964.

Answer:

QUESTION 211

Which contemporary issue in special education is influenced by advances in technology?

- A. The identification of students with disabilities.
- B. The overrepresentation of culturally and linguistically diverse students in special education.
- C. The implementation of inclusion practices in schools.
- D. The development of individualized education plans (IEPs).

Answer:

QUESTION 212

Which trend in special education promotes the best practices for supporting students with disabilities while fostering an inclusive learning environment?

- A. Mainstreaming all students with disabilities into general education classrooms without additional support.
- B. Segregating students with severe disabilities in separate, self-contained classrooms.
- C. Implementing Universal Design for Learning (UDL) principles to meet diverse learning needs.
- D. Using standardized teaching methods for all students regardless of their abilities.

Answer:

QUESTION 213

Mr. Lee is a special education teacher working with young children. He believes early intervention is crucial for children with developmental delays or disabilities. What is the primary rationale behind Mr. Lee's belief?

- A. Early intervention can prevent overrepresentation of certain cultural groups in special education programs.
- B. Early intervention leads to higher funding for special education services in schools.
- C. Early intervention can reduce the need for Individualized Education Plans (IEPs) for students.
- D. Early intervention can lead to improved developmental outcomes and academic success.

Answer:

QUESTION 214

As a dedicated special education teacher, Sarah is always looking for ways to enhance her professional skills and engage in lifelong professional growth. She wants to stay updated with the latest research and best practices in the field. Which of the following activities would be most effective for Sarah to achieve her goals?

- A. Attending workshops and conferences on general education topics.
- B. Joining a local special education teacher association and attending their monthly meetings.
- C. Pursuing a certification in a completely unrelated field to broaden her knowledge.
- D. Participating in online forums and social media groups unrelated to education.

Answer:

QUESTION 215

As a special education teacher, staying informed about current trends and research in the field is essential for maintaining high standards of professional practice. Which of the following resources would be most beneficial for a teacher seeking up-to-date information?

 A. An educational magazine with a focus on general teaching strategies.
 B. A peer-reviewed journal specializing in special education research.
 C. A self-help book on time management and productivity.
 D. A fictional novel that explores themes of diversity and inclusion.

Answer:

QUESTION 216

In order to uphold high standards for professional practice, special education teachers must continuously seek opportunities for growth and development. Which of the following activities demonstrates the most effective approach to professional development?

 A. Attending a one-time, full-day workshop on a specific teaching technique.
 B. Enrolling in a year-long online course covering various topics in special education.
 C. Participating in a brief online webinar on general education trends.
 D. Watching educational videos on a video-sharing platform during leisure time.

Answer:

QUESTION 217

As part of professional growth and development, special education teachers can benefit from collaborating with colleagues and sharing best practices. Which of the following options offers the best platform for such collaboration?

 A. Attending a social gathering with colleagues from various professions.
 B. Participating in an online forum open to the general public.
 C. Joining a specialized professional learning community for special educators.
 D. Volunteering for community events unrelated to education.

Answer:

QUESTION 218

Special education teachers seeking professional growth and development can access various resources to expand their knowledge. Which of the following resources would be most beneficial for self-paced, continuous learning?

 A. Attending an annual national conference on special education.
 B. Subscribing to a monthly online magazine for educators.
 C. Joining a weekly book club focused on literature in general education.
 D. Enrolling in a series of self-paced online courses on special education topics.

Answer:

QUESTION 219

Sarah, a 7-year-old student with autism, has been exhibiting challenging behaviors in the classroom. Her special education teacher has tried various behavior management strategies, but none seem to be effective. The teacher suspects that Sarah's behavior is related to sensory processing difficulties. What should the teacher do next?

A. Consult with the school's behavior specialist to develop a new behavior intervention plan.
B. Implement consequences for each challenging behavior to reduce its occurrence.
C. Request a meeting with Sarah's parents to discuss their parenting techniques at home.
D. Conduct an Individualized Education Program (IEP) review without involving other stakeholders.

Answer:

QUESTION 220

Which of the following scenarios is a potential violation of student confidentiality under the Family Educational Rights and Privacy Act (FERPA)?

A. A special education teacher discusses a student's academic progress with their parents during a parent-teacher conference.
B. A school administrator shares a student's IEP information with a general education teacher who is part of the student's education team.
C. A school counselor provides a student's educational records to their previous school upon request.
D. A special education teacher discusses a student's behavioral challenges with other teachers in the school during a professional development workshop.

Answer:

QUESTION 221

A special education teacher has a student with a specific learning disability who struggles with reading comprehension. The teacher wants to provide the student with an accommodation to support their learning needs. Which accommodation is most appropriate for the student during reading assessments?

A. Providing the student with a summary of the reading passage before the assessment.
B. Allowing the student to take the assessment in a separate, distraction-free room.
C. Permitting the student to have extra time to complete the assessment.
D. Reading the entire assessment aloud to the student.

Answer:

QUESTION 222

James, a 10-year-old student with ADHD, often experiences impulsive behaviors and has difficulty staying seated during classroom activities. He frequently disrupts the class by getting up and walking around. The teacher wants to create an effective behavior plan to support James in managing his impulses. Which strategy should the teacher consider first?

A. Implementing a daily behavior chart to track James's behavior and provide rewards for staying seated.
B. Requesting a meeting with James's parents to discuss their responsibilities in managing his impulsivity.
C. Modifying the classroom environment to include movement breaks and flexible seating options.
D. Referring James to the school counselor for counseling sessions to address his impulsive behaviors.

Answer:

QUESTION 223

A special education teacher is developing an Individualized Education Program (IEP) for a student with a disability. The student's parents have expressed their desire to be actively involved in the decision-making process. How can the teacher best engage the parents in the IEP development?

    A.   Send the completed IEP to the parents for their review and signature.
    B.   Conduct the IEP meeting without inviting the parents to ensure unbiased decision-making.
    C.   Hold a pre-IEP meeting with the parents to discuss their concerns, preferences, and goals for the student.
    D.   Seek input from other teachers and school staff only to avoid potential conflicts with parental preferences.

Answer:

QUESTION 224

As a special education teacher, you recently completed a series of workshops on inclusive teaching practices. After implementing these practices in your classroom, you want to assess your effectiveness and identify areas for improvement. Which self-assessment strategy would be most effective for this purpose?

    A.   Conducting a survey among your students to gather their feedback on the new teaching methods.
    B.   Comparing your students' current academic performance with their performance before implementing inclusive practices.
    C.   Recording video footage of your classroom lessons and reviewing them to analyze your instructional techniques.
    D.   Engaging in peer observation and feedback with another special education teacher who attended the same workshops.

Answer:

QUESTION 225

During a professional development workshop, a special education teacher becomes aware of potential cultural biases that may unintentionally influence their interactions with students from diverse backgrounds. What is the best approach for the teacher to address and mitigate these biases?

    A.   Avoid discussing cultural topics in the classroom to minimize the risk of biases affecting interactions.
    B.   Seek guidance from colleagues who have experience in teaching diverse student populations.
    C.   Embrace the biases as part of personal teaching style and be transparent with students about them.
    D.   Engage in ongoing self-reflection and learning about cultural diversity and its impact on education.

Answer:

QUESTION 226

A special education teacher wants to set meaningful goals for their professional growth. Which approach is likely to be the most effective in this process?

    A.   Setting goals based on the professional standards and requirements set by the school district.
    B.   Choosing goals that require minimal effort to achieve within a short timeframe.
    C.   Seeking input from colleagues and adopting their goals to align with the team's objectives.
    D.   Identifying areas of professional practice that the teacher is passionate about improving.

Answer:

QUESTION 227

As a special education teacher, you have been implementing a new instructional approach for teaching math to students with learning disabilities. After several weeks, you notice that while some students have shown progress, others are still struggling to grasp the concepts. What should you do to improve the effectiveness of your instructional approach?

A. Revert to your previous instructional methods, as they were familiar to the students.
B. Provide the struggling students with additional homework to reinforce the concepts.
C. Assess the individual needs of each student and modify your instructional approach accordingly.
D. Request to switch students between different special education classrooms to balance the learning levels.

Answer:

QUESTION 228

A special education teacher has been engaged in reflection and self-assessment activities to identify areas of improvement in their teaching practice. What should the teacher do after identifying specific areas for growth?

A. Create an action plan with clear, measurable goals and a timeline for improvement.
B. Share the identified weaknesses with colleagues to seek validation and feedback.
C. Compare their performance with other special education teachers to gauge their standing.
D. Ignore the areas of weakness and focus solely on enhancing existing strengths.

Answer:

QUESTION 229

What is the primary responsibility of a special education teacher in an inclusive classroom setting?

A. Design and implement specialized instructional strategies for students with disabilities.
B. Support the general education teacher in managing classroom behavior.
C. Prepare individualized education plans (IEPs) for all students in the class.
D. Assess and grade students' academic performance.

Answer:

QUESTION 230

A special education teacher receives a new student with a learning disability in the middle of the academic year. What is the most appropriate first step for the teacher to take?

A. Request the student's previous individualized education plan (IEP) from the previous school.
B. Conduct an initial assessment to identify the student's strengths and weaknesses.
C. Introduce the student to the rest of the class and assign a buddy to help with the transition.
D. Provide the student with grade-level materials and observe their performance in class.

Answer:

QUESTION 231

In a case where a special education teacher disagrees with the goals outlined in a student's Individualized Education Plan (IEP), what should be the teacher's immediate course of action?

    A.   Follow the IEP as it is a legally binding document.
    B.   Consult with the school principal to request an IEP review meeting.
    C.   Contact the student's parents to discuss the teacher's concerns.
    D.   Implement alternative goals based on the teacher's professional judgment.

Answer:

QUESTION 232

Which of the following is a crucial aspect of collaboration between a special education teacher and a general education teacher in an inclusive classroom?

    A.   The general education teacher should solely handle all students' behavior management.
    B.   The special education teacher should provide all instructional materials and resources.
    C.   Both teachers should share responsibility for planning and delivering instruction.
    D.   The special education teacher should focus only on students with disabilities.

Answer:

QUESTION 233

A special education teacher is working with a student who has a specific learning disability in reading comprehension. Despite various interventions, the student's progress is minimal. What should the teacher do next?

    A.   Request a transfer for the student to a different class.
    B.   Continue with the current interventions, as progress may take time.
    C.   Seek assistance from a reading specialist or educational psychologist.
    D.   Modify the student's IEP to include more straightforward reading materials.

Answer:

QUESTION 234

Ms. Johnson, a special education teacher, recently attended a professional development workshop on culturally responsive teaching. After reflecting on her teaching practices, she realizes that she tends to overlook cultural differences in her classroom. What is the most appropriate next step for Ms. Johnson?

    A.   Ignore the realization and continue with her current teaching methods.
    B.   Seek feedback from her colleagues about their cultural practices in the classroom.
    C.   Develop a plan to incorporate culturally responsive teaching strategies in her instruction.
    D.   Enroll in a course on classroom management to improve her teaching skills.

Answer:

QUESTION 235

As part of self-assessment, a special education teacher identifies a weakness in managing classroom behavior effectively, especially during transitions. What should be the teacher's next course of action?

A. Avoid transitions in the classroom to minimize behavior issues.
B. Seek assistance from a behavioral specialist to manage transitions.
C. Observe other experienced teachers to learn effective transition techniques.
D. Create a behavior management plan with strategies to address transitions.

Answer:

QUESTION 236

A special education teacher wants to set meaningful goals for professional growth. Which approach would be most effective for this purpose?

A. Select goals that require minimal effort to achieve for a sense of accomplishment.
B. Base goals on the strengths of the teacher to reinforce existing abilities.
C. Set goals that align with the school's requirements to ensure compliance.
D. Identify areas of improvement and set challenging, yet achievable, goals.

Answer:

QUESTION 237

Mr. Rodriguez, a special education teacher, is committed to improving his teaching strategies and meeting the needs of his diverse students. After reflecting on his performance, he believes he needs to enhance his understanding of instructional technology to better engage his students. What would be the most effective step for Mr. Rodriguez to take next?

A. Stick to traditional teaching methods, as technology might not be suitable for all students.
B. Enroll in a general technology course to learn the basics of instructional technology.
C. Attend workshops or webinars specifically focused on using technology in special education.
D. Request the school administration to assign a technology assistant for his classroom.

Answer:

QUESTION 238

A special education teacher regularly engages in self-reflection to identify strengths and weaknesses in instruction. However, the teacher finds it challenging to remain objective and struggles with critical self-assessment. What would be the most appropriate solution for this situation?

A. Discontinue self-reflection as it may lead to self-doubt.
B. Seek feedback from students and parents to gain external perspectives.
C. Compare instructional practices with other teachers to establish benchmarks.
D. Enroll in a professional development course on self-assessment and reflection.

Answer:

QUESTION 239

You are a special education teacher working with a student who has a learning disability and comes from a culturally diverse background. The student's parent speaks limited English and feels disconnected from their child's education. What is the most effective strategy to address this situation and improve communication with the parent?

    A. Send written communication in English, assuming the parent can understand basic information.
    B. Use a professional interpreter during parent-teacher conferences and important meetings.
    C. Request the parent to learn English to enhance communication with school staff.
    D. Avoid involving the parent in the education process to prevent misunderstandings.

Answer:

QUESTION 240

Which of the following approaches is best for fostering a positive and inclusive classroom environment for students with disabilities from diverse cultural and linguistic backgrounds?

    A. Segregating students with disabilities during class activities.
    B. Using standardized assessments without accommodations for diverse learners.
    C. Incorporating culturally responsive teaching practices and providing appropriate accommodations.
    D. Avoiding collaboration with parents from diverse cultural backgrounds.

Answer:

QUESTION 241

You have a student with a visual impairment in your class. The student's parents are concerned about their child's learning outcomes and want to be actively involved in the education process. What is the most appropriate way to collaborate with the parents?

    A. Minimize parental involvement to maintain a professional boundary.
    B. Provide information and updates to parents in written form only.
    C. Organize regular meetings with the parents, involving them in the decision-making process.
    D. Encourage the parents to seek support from other parents of visually impaired children.

Answer:

QUESTION 242

Which of the following strategies is most effective for promoting positive communication between a special education teacher and a parent who speaks a different language?

    A. Relying on nonverbal cues to communicate effectively.
    B. Using machine translation apps or online tools without involving an interpreter.
    C. Encouraging the parent to communicate in English to improve language proficiency.
    D. Utilizing a trained bilingual interpreter for accurate and sensitive communication.

Answer:

QUESTION 243

You have a student with a specific learning disability who comes from a culturally diverse background. The student's parent expresses concerns about their child's progress and asks for ways to support learning at home. What is the most appropriate recommendation?

A. Provide the parent with a list of private tutors who specialize in working with students with learning disabilities.
B. Suggest the parent to enroll the child in extracurricular activities to enhance their learning abilities.
C. Share specific strategies and resources tailored to the child's learning needs that the parent can use at home.
D. Advise the parent to focus on discipline and setting stricter study routines for the child.

Answer:

QUESTION 244

Which of the following methods is most effective for communicating with a non-verbal student who uses augmentative and alternative communication (AAC) devices?

A. Speaking to the student's classmates about important class updates.
B. Communicating through written notes or emails sent to the student's parent.
C. Utilizing the AAC device and allowing adequate response time for the student.
D. Assuming the student does not understand and seeking alternative solutions.

Answer:

QUESTION 245

You are conducting a parent-teacher conference with the parent of a student with autism spectrum disorder (ASD). The parent appears disengaged and overwhelmed by the information being discussed. What should you do to improve communication during the conference?

A. Continue providing all the necessary information, assuming the parent will understand eventually.
B. Offer the parent a written summary of the discussion to review later at their own pace.
C. Use complex educational jargon and terminology to maintain professionalism.
D. Pause frequently to check for the parent's understanding and provide information in a clear and accessible manner.

Answer:

QUESTION 246

What is the most effective strategy for collaborating with general education teachers to support the learning outcomes of students with disabilities in an inclusive classroom?

A. Encourage the general education teachers to handle all aspects of students' education independently.
B. Provide the general education teachers with minimal information about the students' disabilities to maintain privacy.
C. Organize regular meetings to discuss individual students' needs and develop collaborative strategies.
D. Suggest the general education teachers focus solely on academic progress and not on social inclusion.

Answer:

Chapter 2 – Answers and Explanations

QUESTION 1

Answer: B

Explanation: Given Sarah's diagnosis of Down syndrome and her challenges with communication, multi-step instructions, and anxiety, the most appropriate approach is to develop an Individualized Education Plan (IEP) that addresses her unique needs. An IEP is a personalized plan designed to support students with disabilities, outlining specific goals, accommodations, and interventions to help them succeed academically and socially. By tailoring the plan to focus on communication and social skills development, Sarah can receive targeted support and achieve better progress.

QUESTION 2

Answer: C

Explanation: Students diagnosed with ADHD typically exhibit symptoms of impulsivity, inattention, and hyperactivity. These students may struggle with maintaining focus, act without thinking, have difficulty organizing tasks, and show excessive restlessness or fidgeting. It is essential for special education teachers to recognize these characteristics to provide appropriate support and interventions to help these students succeed in their academic and social environments.

QUESTION 3

Answer: C

Explanation: In supporting Alex's strengths and addressing his challenges, it is essential to consider both aspects of his needs. While his interest in computer programming should be encouraged and nurtured, it is also crucial to work on improving his social interactions. Developing a social skills group will provide Alex with a structured and supportive environment to practice and develop social communication, understanding emotions, and building relationships with peers. By addressing his social challenges, he can enhance his overall well-being and be better equipped to navigate social situations in various settings.

QUESTION 4

Answer: C

Explanation: Students with specific learning disabilities face challenges in acquiring certain academic skills despite having average to above-average intelligence in other areas. These difficulties can manifest in areas such as reading, writing, math, or other academic domains. It is important for special education teachers to identify and address these specific learning needs through targeted interventions and accommodations to help these students succeed academically.

QUESTION 5

Answer: C

Explanation: To support Mark's learning and boost his self-esteem, it is important to focus on his strengths and interests, in this case, his creativity and talent in arts and crafts. By providing opportunities for him to engage in arts-related projects, you can tap into his passion and allow him to experience success and recognition in areas where he excels. This positive reinforcement can have a significant impact on his self-confidence and overall well-being. Additionally, it's crucial to address his reading difficulties through appropriate interventions and support, but not at the expense of neglecting his strengths and passions.

QUESTION 6

Answer: C

Explanation: Inclusivity is essential in education, and it is important to provide Jenny with equal opportunities to participate in physical education classes. Modifying the activities to accommodate her mobility challenges and providing adaptive equipment that suits her needs, such as specialized wheelchairs or adapted sports equipment, can enable her to actively engage and enjoy physical activities with her peers. It's crucial to foster a supportive and inclusive environment that values diversity and ensures that all students, regardless of their disabilities, can participate in educational activities to the best of their abilities.

QUESTION 7

Answer: B

Explanation: Nonverbal learning disability (NVLD) is characterized by difficulties in processing nonverbal information and cues. As a result, individuals with NVLD may struggle to understand and interpret nonverbal cues and body language, which are crucial aspects of social interactions. This can lead to challenges in forming and maintaining social relationships, as they may have difficulty picking up on social cues, facial expressions, and gestures that are essential for effective communication and social bonding.

QUESTION 8

Answer: D

Explanation: Transitioning to post-secondary education is a significant milestone for students, and it's essential to ensure that Mark's needs are adequately supported. Instead of discouraging him from pursuing higher education or solely focusing on academics, the most appropriate approach is to collaborate with post-secondary institutions to provide necessary accommodations that address his sensory challenges. By working with disability support services at these institutions, you can help create an environment that accommodates his sensory needs, such as providing quieter study spaces or allowing for flexibility in course selections. This collaboration will increase Mark's chances of succeeding in his chosen academic path.

QUESTION 9

Answer: D

Explanation: Specific learning disabilities (SLDs) can affect various aspects of an individual's life, including their employment opportunities. People with SLDs may face challenges in understanding and following written or verbal instructions accurately, which can impact their job performance and productivity. It is essential for special education teachers to work with students with SLDs to develop strategies and accommodations that can support their learning and functional skills, enabling them to succeed in the workplace.

QUESTION 10

Answer: B

Explanation: Empowering Linda for independent living means equipping her with the necessary tools and resources to overcome her challenges. Instead of discouraging her or relying solely on others to handle reading tasks, providing Linda with audio-based resources and assistive technologies can be transformative. These accommodations will enable her to access information, read texts, and navigate written materials independently. With access to audio-based resources, Linda can enhance her independence and engage more effectively in various aspects of independent living, including managing her daily activities, accessing information, and pursuing her goals.

QUESTION 11

Answer: D

Explanation: During early childhood, typically developing children show a decrease in egocentrism, meaning they become better at understanding others' perspectives and experiences. This is a significant milestone in social development. Option A is incorrect because logical reasoning and abstract thinking skills are still developing during this stage and are not fully matured. Option B is incorrect because memory capabilities continue to improve but are not yet fully developed. Option C is incorrect because symbolic play and imaginative thinking are more prominent during early childhood.

QUESTION 12

Answer: C

Explanation: For a child with atypical speech and language development, especially one who is mostly nonverbal, implementing augmentative and alternative communication (AAC) strategies is essential. AAC tools, such as picture symbols or communication devices, can aid in enhancing communication and language development for nonverbal or minimally verbal individuals. Option A is incorrect because expecting the child to speak in full sentences may be beyond their current communication abilities and might cause frustration. Option B is incorrect because relying solely on flashcards and worksheets may not be effective for a child with significant language delays. Option D is incorrect because frequent corrections of pronunciation and grammar errors might discourage the child from attempting to communicate and hinder their language development.

QUESTION 13

Answer: C

Explanation: During adolescence, individuals are more susceptible to peer pressure and conformity. This is a characteristic of typical social/emotional development as they strive to fit in and be accepted by their peers. Option A is incorrect because mood swings and emotional variability are common during adolescence. Option B is incorrect because a typical adolescent seeks more independence from their caregivers as they strive for autonomy. Option D is incorrect because adolescence is a period of significant self-exploration and identity formation, often leading to questioning and challenging aspects of their self-identity.

QUESTION 14

Answer: C

Explanation: The child's difficulty maintaining attention, fidgeting, interrupting others, and struggling to wait their turn are characteristic symptoms of Attention-deficit/hyperactivity disorder (ADHD). These behaviors have been present for at least six months and significantly impact the child's academic performance and social interactions, which align with the diagnostic criteria for ADHD. Option A is incorrect because specific learning disabilities in reading would primarily affect the child's reading abilities and may not explain the other behaviors mentioned. Option B is incorrect because Oppositional defiant disorder (ODD) is characterized by a pattern of angry, defiant, and vindictive behavior, which does not fully align with the described behaviors. Option D is incorrect because Autism spectrum disorder (ASD) is associated with difficulties in social communication, repetitive behaviors, and restricted interests, but it does not fully explain the attention-related and hyperactive behaviors observed in this case.

QUESTION 15

Answer: C

Explanation: For a student with a specific learning disability and seizures, the most appropriate medication option is Levetiracetam (Keppra) to manage seizure activity. Levetiracetam is an antiepileptic drug used to treat various types of seizures, including absence seizures (characterized by brief periods of staring and subtle body movements). Options A, B, and D are not relevant to seizure management and may not be suitable for this student's specific medical needs.

QUESTION 16

Answer: C

Explanation: Medication administration in the school setting for students with disabilities requires proper documentation and confidentiality. School staff, including teachers, may need special training and authorization to administer prescription medications to students. Over-the-counter medications should only be given with appropriate parental consent. Self-administration of medications by students should be done under supervision and based on the school's policy and the student's individual capabilities.

QUESTION 17

Answer: C

Explanation: For a student with cerebral palsy experiencing muscle spasticity, the most appropriate medication option is Baclofen (Lioresal). Baclofen is a muscle relaxant commonly used to manage spasticity, reducing muscle stiffness and improving mobility. Options A, B, and D are not relevant to managing spasticity and may not address the student's primary medical need.

QUESTION 18

Answer: C

Explanation: The role of a special education teacher does not involve diagnosing medical conditions or prescribing medications (Option A). Determining the dosage and frequency of medications is the responsibility of medical professionals (Option B). Special education teachers play a vital role in collaborating with parents, medical professionals, and school staff to ensure that medication administration is safe, appropriate, and meets the individual needs of students with disabilities (Option C). Administering medications directly to students is typically the responsibility of school nurses or other designated staff (Option D).

QUESTION 19

Answer: A

Explanation: The correct answer is (a) Intellectual Disability; Strength in Artistic Abilities. Sarah's difficulties with understanding complex math problems and her enjoyment of drawing and coloring indicate characteristics of Intellectual Disability. Her artistic abilities are a strength often seen in individuals with Down syndrome.

QUESTION 20

Answer: C

Explanation: The correct answer is (c) Specific Learning Disability. Students with a Specific Learning Disability have ongoing challenges in reading and/or writing, even though they have average intelligence and have received appropriate instruction.

QUESTION 21

Answer: C

Explanation: The correct answer is (c) Autism Spectrum Disorder; Sensory Overload. Jason's behaviors of becoming agitated and displaying aggressive behavior in response to changes in routine or environment are characteristic of individuals with autism. Sensory overload is often a primary trigger for such reactions in individuals with autism.

QUESTION 22

Answer: C

Explanation: The correct answer is (c) Speech and Language Impairment. This disability category involves difficulties in communication, including challenges with speech articulation and language comprehension.

QUESTION 23

Answer: D

Explanation: The correct answer is (d) Written Expression. Emma's challenges in expressing herself in writing and frequently misspelling words are indicative of difficulties in written expression, which is an area that the special education teacher should focus on to support her needs.

QUESTION 24

Answer: C

Explanation: Since Sarah is facing specific challenges in reading, collaborating with the speech therapist is crucial. Language processing issues could be contributing to her struggles in decoding and comprehension. The speech therapist can assess her language skills and provide targeted interventions to address any underlying language difficulties, which will support her overall reading development.

QUESTION 25

Answer: A

Explanation: Socioeconomic status plays a crucial role in the daily living skills development of students with intellectual disabilities. A lower socioeconomic status may limit access to resources, specialized services, and opportunities for skill-building. In contrast, students from higher socioeconomic backgrounds may have better access to support and opportunities, which can positively influence their development of daily living skills.

QESTION 26

Answer: B

Explanation: Since Jason shows great interest and positive responses to music, incorporating it into various learning activities across the curriculum can be highly beneficial. Music can serve as a motivating and engaging tool to enhance his participation, attention, and memory across different subjects and tasks, facilitating his overall learning and development.

QUESTION 27

Answer: D

Explanation: An inclusive approach aims to ensure that all students, regardless of their abilities or disabilities, can fully participate and benefit from classroom activities. By creating activities that accommodate the needs of all students, educators foster a supportive and accepting environment where every learner can thrive and contribute to the learning process.

QUESTION 28

Answer: C

Explanation: Providing written or visual cues can be an effective accommodation to support Emma's time management and focus. These cues can include visual schedules, timers, and reminders, helping her stay organized and manage her time effectively. Reducing her workload or allowing her to skip lectures may not address the core challenges she faces in staying focused and managing her time, whereas visual cues cater directly to her specific needs.

QUESTION 29

Answer: D

Explanation: Encouraging Alex to use a computer for writing tasks can significantly support his participation and independence. A computer enables him to type, which is often a more accessible method for students with fine motor challenges. It empowers Alex to express his thoughts and ideas without the limitations of handwriting, promoting his overall academic engagement and success.

QUESTION 30

Answer: A

Explanation: Exposure to social skills training programs can significantly impact the development of social skills in students with autism spectrum disorder. These programs provide structured interventions and strategies to teach essential social skills, such as communication, emotional regulation, and social interaction. With targeted training, students with ASD can improve their social competencies and better navigate social situations, enhancing their overall social development.

QUESTION 31

Answer: C

Explanation: Conducting a comprehensive evaluation is crucial to identify the specific areas of difficulty in Maria's mathematics learning. This evaluation can help pinpoint her learning gaps and provide insights into the most effective interventions for her needs. A tailored approach based on the evaluation results will offer targeted support, addressing her challenges and promoting progress in mathematics.

QUESTION 32

Answer: C

Explanation: Using tactile graphics and braille alongside printed text ensures accessibility for students with visual impairments. Tactile graphics allow students to "feel" images and diagrams, making visual information accessible through touch. Additionally, providing braille versions of written content allows students to read the materials independently. By combining tactile and braille adaptations, educators create an inclusive learning environment where students with visual impairments can access the same information as their sighted peers.

QUESTION 33

Answer: C

Explanation: Allowing students to take an active role in setting their goals promotes self-determination. Self-determination refers to the ability to make choices, set personal goals, and take responsibility for one's actions and decisions. By involving students in the goal-setting process, educators empower them to develop their decision-making skills and take ownership of their learning journey. This fosters a sense of autonomy and self-confidence, which are essential for long-term success and independence in students with disabilities.

QUESTION 34

Answer: D

Explanation: Given the parents' busy work schedules, it might be challenging for them to actively participate in school committees or volunteer for events. Option D offers a practical and considerate approach by accommodating their availability through alternative communication methods like emails or virtual meetings. This way, the teacher can ensure effective communication and collaboration with Sarah's parents despite their time constraints.

QUESTION 35

Answer: B

Explanation: Option B is the correct choice because it promotes cultural competence and sensitivity. Collaborating with the school's multicultural liaison allows the special education teacher to gain insights into David's cultural background, values, and traditions, enabling them to create a supportive and inclusive learning environment that respects his family's unique customs without making assumptions or implementing strategies solely based on stereotypes.

QUESTION 36

Answer: C

Explanation: Option C is the correct choice because creating a safe and supportive environment in the classroom fosters trust between the teacher, Lily, and her classmates. When students feel comfortable sharing their challenges without the fear of judgment or disappointment, they are more likely to communicate openly with both the teacher and their parents. This approach can help Lily feel supported and encouraged to discuss her academic struggles with her parents.

QUESTION 37

Answer: C

Explanation: Option C is the correct choice as it promotes active involvement and collaboration between the parents and the teacher. Parent-teacher conferences provide a structured setting where Mark's parents can discuss his progress, learning strategies, and any specific concerns related to his ADHD. Encouraging them to share their suggestions during these meetings allows the teacher to understand Mark's needs better and work together to support his development and learning effective.

QUESTION 38

Answer: B

Explanation: Option B is the correct choice as it empowers Emma's parents with knowledge and tools to better support her learning and development outside of the school setting. By providing resources about visual impairment and relevant strategies, the teacher equips Emma's parents with valuable information to create an inclusive and supportive environment at home, which can positively impact her overall educational experience.

QUESTION 39

Answer: A

Explanation: Option A is the correct choice as it demonstrates cultural sensitivity and ensures effective communication between the school and Ethan's family. Providing translated materials and interpreters during school events allows Ethan's family to actively engage in his education without language barriers, ensuring they receive necessary information and can participate in discussions and decision-making processes related to his development and learning.

QUESTION 40

Answer: B

Explanation: Option B is the correct choice as it promotes transparent communication and collaboration between the teacher and James's parents. Providing regular progress reports and academic assessments keeps the parents informed about James's performance, strengths, and areas that need improvement. This information empowers the parents to actively participate in his educational journey and make informed decisions regarding appropriate interventions and support.

QUESTION 41

Answer: A

Explanation: Option A is the correct choice as it suggests a proactive approach to enhance Mia's social interactions. Enrolling Mia in extracurricular activities allows her to interact with peers in a less structured setting, giving her opportunities to develop and practice her social skills in various contexts. Additionally, participating in activities of interest can boost her self-confidence and foster positive relationships with peers outside the classroom environment.

QUESTION 42

Answer: B

Explanation: The student's difficulty in decoding unfamiliar words and displaying slow and inaccurate reading suggests a deficit in reading skills. Option B, implementing a multisensory reading program that focuses on phonics and decoding skills, directly targets the student's needs and is an evidence-based intervention for students with learning disabilities in reading.

QUESTION 43

Answer: C

Explanation: Ongoing assessments in special education serve the purpose of monitoring students' progress, identifying areas of growth and challenges, and guiding the teacher in making informed instructional decisions. This allows the teacher to tailor the program and interventions to meet the student's individual needs effectively.

QUESTION 44

Answer: D

Explanation: The Childhood Autism Rating Scale (CARS) is designed to assess the severity of autism spectrum disorder in children. It evaluates behaviors related to social interaction, communication, and repetitive behaviors, making it the most appropriate tool for gathering information about the student's specific communication and social interaction challenges in this case.

QUESTION 45

Answer: C

Explanation: When creating an Individualized Education Program (IEP), it is essential to involve key stakeholders who have direct knowledge of the student and their educational needs. This includes the student's parents or guardians, the general education teacher, and relevant specialists, such as speech therapists, occupational therapists, or other professionals who can contribute valuable insights into the student's abilities and challenges.

QUESTION 46

Answer: D

Explanation: Formative assessment is an ongoing process that occurs during the learning journey. Its primary purpose is to provide continuous feedback to both teachers and students about progress and understanding. In special education, formative assessment plays a crucial role in guiding instructional decisions and adapting teaching strategies to meet the individual needs of the student.

QUESTION 47

Answer: C

Explanation: The student's struggles with understanding fractions indicate a specific learning disability in mathematics. Option C, implementing a systematic, research-based intervention targeting the understanding of fractions, directly addresses the identified area of need. It allows for targeted instruction and provides the student with the support required to make progress in this specific area.

QUESTION 48

Answer: C

Explanation: Formative assessment data provides ongoing feedback and insight into a student's progress and understanding. Option C, using formative assessment data to identify a student's strengths and weaknesses and adjusting instruction accordingly, aligns with the purpose of formative assessments in improving instruction and interventions to meet individual student needs.

QUESTION 49

A special education teacher is working with a student who has attention deficit hyperactivity disorder (ADHD) and exhibits impulsive behavior in the classroom. The student often interrupts others during discussions and has difficulty waiting for their turn. Which assessment tool would be most helpful in gathering data to address the student's impulsive behavior?

Answer: A

Explanation: The Behavior Assessment System for Children (BASC-3) is designed to assess various aspects of a child's behavior, including attention and hyperactivity. It provides valuable information about the student's impulsive behavior and can guide the development of targeted behavior intervention strategies.

QUESTION 50

Answer: B

Explanation: Involving parents in the educational process is essential, especially for students with ASD. Option B, reviewing the assessment data with the parents and involving them in creating a personalized education plan, ensures a collaborative approach that considers the student's strengths, weaknesses, and individual needs to develop effective interventions and support.

QUESTION 51

Answer: D

Explanation: A significant discrepancy between cognitive abilities and academic achievement is often indicative of a specific learning disability. Option D, considering appropriate academic interventions, is the appropriate next step. Further assessment and intervention planning should focus on addressing the specific learning challenges the student is experiencing.

QUESTION 52

Answer: C

Explanation: When developing an IEP, it is essential to consider the individual student's strengths and weaknesses, as well as their present levels of academic performance. These factors help identify areas of need and guide the selection of appropriate goals and objectives that are tailored to the student's specific learning disability in written expression.

QUESTION 53

Answer: D

Explanation: Measurable goals and objectives in an IEP or other individualized plans allow for progress monitoring and assessment of the student's performance over time. It enables teachers to track the effectiveness of interventions and make data-driven decisions to support the student's academic growth.

QUESTION 54

Answer: C

Explanation: For a student with ASD struggling with social interactions and communication, the use of visual supports and social stories can be effective in improving social understanding and promoting appropriate social behaviors. Option C aligns with evidence-based practices for supporting students with autism.

QUESTION 55

Answer: B

Explanation: When setting annual goals for an IEP or other individualized plans, it is important to strike a balance between challenging the student to make progress and ensuring the goals are realistic based on the student's current abilities. Option B focuses on setting goals that are both attainable and meaningful for the individual student.

QUESTION 56

Answer: B

Explanation: The development of an IEP or other individualized plans requires a collaborative team approach. Option B includes key stakeholders who have direct knowledge of the student's abilities and challenges, including the student's parents or guardians, the general education teacher, and relevant specialists such as therapists or counselors. Their input and expertise are crucial in creating effective and comprehensive plans to meet the student's individual needs.

QUESTION 57

Answer: B

Explanation: In this case, Mr. Johnson should modify the informal assessment to accommodate the student's speech difficulties. By providing written comprehension questions, the student can respond in writing or select multiple-choice answers, which better suits their needs and removes the discomfort associated with verbal responses. The modification ensures the assessment is fair and aligned with the student's abilities.

QUESTION 58

Answer: B

Explanation: In this situation, providing the visually impaired student with an audio version of the standardized test is the most appropriate solution. This modification allows the student to listen to the questions, ensuring that their visual impairment doesn't hinder their mathematical assessment. Providing equal access to the assessment is crucial to obtaining accurate results for the student's mathematical abilities.

QUESTION 59

Answer: C

Explanation: When a student performs below grade level on a standardized writing test, it is essential to gain a deeper understanding of their specific writing difficulties. By using an informal writing assessment, the teacher can tailor the prompts and tasks to the student's needs, gather more detailed information, and identify specific areas of concern. This will help the teacher create targeted interventions and support the student's writing development effectively.

QUESTION 60

Answer: A

Explanation: To address the challenges posed by the student's ADHD during the assessment, providing additional breaks to allow the student to move around is a helpful modification. These breaks can help the student release restlessness and improve focus when they return to the assessment tasks. Shortening the assessment or eliminating it altogether may not provide an accurate picture of the student's mathematical abilities, and changing the format to focus on oral questioning may not fully address the student's challenges.

QUESTION 61

Answer: D

Explanation: When assessing the reading comprehension skills of a student with ASD who exhibits difficulty understanding written text, using an interactive reading assessment with audio support is an effective approach. The audio support can help the student by providing verbal cues and explanations, enhancing their understanding of the text. This modification aligns with the student's needs and ensures a more accurate assessment of their reading comprehension skills.

QUESTION 62

Answer: D

Explanation: To develop an effective IEP for the student with learning disabilities, Ms. Adams should address the student's areas of difficulty comprehensively. Including specific and measurable goals for both reading comprehension and written expression ensures that the IEP is tailored to the student's individual needs. Focusing solely on reading comprehension or using a one-size-fits-all approach may not adequately support the student's overall academic growth.

QUESTION 63

Answer: C

Explanation: To make informed decisions about the progress of an individualized program for a student with intellectual disabilities, the special education teacher should collect data related to the student's individualized goals and objectives. This data provides insights into the student's specific areas of improvement or challenges. Relying solely on mainstream classroom assignments or anecdotal notes may not accurately reflect the student's progress toward their targeted goals.

QUESTION 64

Answer: C

Explanation: To address the student's challenging behavior during mathematics class, Mr. Rodriguez should observe the student during these sessions to identify specific triggers that may be contributing to the behavior. Understanding the triggers will help him tailor the behavior intervention plan to address the student's needs effectively. Implementing the BIP consistently across all subjects is essential, but identifying triggers specific to mathematics class will enable Mr. Rodriguez to make targeted interventions.

QUESTION 65

Answer: C

Explanation: Considering the student's interests and strengths when developing an individualized program for a student with autism spectrum disorder is significant because it enhances the student's motivation and engagement in learning activities. Tailoring the program to align with the student's interests helps create a positive learning environment, fostering a sense of enjoyment and curiosity in the student. This motivation can lead to increased participation and improved overall learning outcomes.

QUESTION 66

Answer: C

Explanation: Involving parents or guardians in the development and implementation of an individualized program is essential for its success. Scheduling regular meetings to discuss the student's progress and goals collaboratively allows parents to actively participate in their child's education and provide valuable insights about their strengths, weaknesses, and preferences. This collaborative approach ensures that the program is well-aligned with the student's needs and fosters a supportive partnership between the teacher and parents.

QUESTION 67

Answer: C

Explanation: To enhance the student's integration into the general education program, Ms. Johnson should collaborate with the general education teacher to implement targeted accommodations. These accommodations can include providing additional time for assignments and assessments, offering preferential seating, or using assistive technology. This way, the student can continue benefiting from the general education environment while receiving the necessary supports to succeed.

QUESTION 68

Answer: B

Explanation: For a student with emotional and behavioral disorders who has difficulty maintaining appropriate behavior in a mainstream classroom setting, the most appropriate placement to consider would be a self-contained special education classroom with a smaller student-to-teacher ratio. This environment can provide the necessary behavioral support and individualized attention, allowing the student to focus on their specific needs and progress at their own pace.

QUESTION 69

Answer: C

Explanation: When planning the continuum of services for students with disabilities, a special education teacher should primarily consider the specific needs and strengths of the students with disabilities. Each student is unique, and their individualized education program (IEP) should be tailored to address their specific requirements for academic, social, and emotional development. This person-centered approach ensures that students receive the appropriate level of support to enhance their learning outcomes.

QUESTION 70

Answer: C

Explanation: To enhance integration and collaboration among students with different disabilities, Mr. Davis should encourage regular group discussions and activities that foster teamwork and empathy. Grouping students based on their disability type (option a) may isolate them and hinder integration. Designating a student leader (option b) may create a power dynamic that could lead to resentment. Providing individual tasks (option d) might limit opportunities for peer interaction. On the other hand, promoting group discussions and activities creates an inclusive environment that encourages students to work together, understand each other's perspectives, and build meaningful connections.

QUESTION 71

Answer: D

Explanation: To support the integration of a student with physical disabilities into the general education program, the special education teacher should consider installing ramps and other accessibility features in the classroom and school premises. These physical accommodations enable the student to move around independently and access various areas of the school without barriers. Providing a personal aide (option a) may not promote independence, and implementing a separate curriculum (option b) may isolate the student from their peers. While offering materials in audio format (option c) is beneficial, ensuring physical accessibility is crucial for the student's overall integration and participation in school activities.

QUESTION 72

Answer: B

Explanation: Curriculum-based assessment (CBA) involves directly assessing a student's performance in the context of their current curriculum. It focuses on measuring a student's progress in relation to the specific skills and knowledge taught in the classroom. CBA is particularly valuable for special education teachers because it allows them to identify a student's individual strengths and weaknesses and make targeted instructional decisions based on the results.

QUESTION 73

Answer: B

Explanation: A portfolio assessment is a collection of a student's work samples over time, which can include written assignments, projects, and other assessments. This type of assessment would be most appropriate in this case because it allows Mrs. Adams to gather evidence of the student's reading comprehension skills through various means, reducing the focus on oral expression and anxiety. The portfolio approach offers flexibility and accommodates the student's learning needs and preferences.

QUESTION 74

Answer: A

Explanation: Standardized tests are designed to be administered and scored in a consistent and uniform manner, ensuring that all students answer the same questions under the same conditions. These assessments are norm-referenced, which means they provide data to compare a student's performance to that of a representative sample of their peers. Standardized tests are commonly used for large-scale assessments and to compare students' abilities on a national or state level.

QUESTION 75

Answer: B

Explanation: An anecdotal record is a type of informal assessment where the observer (in this case, Mr. Johnson) takes notes on specific behaviors, skills, or interactions of the student during a particular activity. It provides valuable qualitative data about the student's performance, strengths, and areas needing improvement. In this scenario, Mr. Johnson is using an anecdotal record to capture the student's math skills and behaviors during math activities.

QUESTION 76

Answer: D

Explanation: Augmentative and Alternative Communication (AAC) is a system that supports or enhances a person's communication abilities, particularly for individuals with limited speech. In this case, an AAC-based assessment would be most appropriate for the student, as it would provide the means to express their understanding of science concepts through alternative methods like picture-based communication systems, communication boards, or assistive technology devices. This approach ensures that the student's communication limitations do not hinder their ability to demonstrate their knowledge and comprehension.

QUESTION 77

Answer: A

Explanation: After conducting initial screenings and interventions, if the student's difficulties persist and there are concerns about their progress, the next appropriate step is to refer the student for a comprehensive evaluation. This evaluation will involve gathering information from various sources to determine if the student meets the eligibility criteria for special education services. It will help identify any specific learning disabilities or other issues that may be impacting the student's academic performance, allowing for more targeted and individualized support.

QUESTION 78

Answer: C

Explanation: The prereferral intervention process is a proactive and collaborative approach where teachers, parents, and other professionals work together to address a student's academic or behavioral difficulties within the general education setting. It involves implementing targeted strategies and interventions to support the student's needs before considering a formal special education evaluation. The goal is to provide early and effective support to potentially prevent the need for special education services.

QUESTION 79

Answer: B

Explanation: The primary purpose of conducting a screening process for students is to identify those who may be at risk for academic or behavioral difficulties. Screening helps to quickly and efficiently identify students who may need additional support and intervention. It is an essential first step in the assessment process and allows educators to address concerns early on to improve students' overall academic and behavioral outcomes.

QUESTION 80

Answer: A

Explanation: In the referral process for a special education evaluation, obtaining consent from the parents or legal guardians of the student is an essential and legally required step. Before conducting any evaluations or assessments, schools must seek written consent from the parents or guardians to ensure they are informed about the process and have the opportunity to be involved in decision-making regarding their child's education.

QUESTION 81

Answer: B

Explanation: When receiving a referral for a new student, the most appropriate initial step for Ms. Hernandez is to request Daniel's previous school records. These records may include academic assessments, progress reports, and any previous interventions or special education services received. Reviewing this information will provide valuable insight into Daniel's academic history and help guide the next steps, such as implementing targeted interventions or conducting a comprehensive evaluation if needed.

QUESTION 82

Answer: C

Explanation: The most appropriate approach for Mr. Davis is to incorporate visual schedules and checklists into the academic curriculum. Visual supports can help students with disabilities improve their organizational skills and time management by providing clear and explicit guidelines for their daily tasks and activities. By integrating these strategies into the academic curriculum, Mr. Davis ensures that students are practicing organizational skills within the context of their regular classwork, making it more relevant and meaningful for them.

QUESTION 83

Answer: A

Explanation: When prioritizing areas of the general curriculum for students with disabilities, special education teachers should consider the students' strengths and interests. Tailoring the curriculum to align with what students are passionate about and where they have natural abilities can increase engagement and motivation. It also enhances the potential for meaningful learning experiences and better overall academic outcomes.

QUESTION 84

Answer: A

Explanation: Voice recognition software would be the most appropriate assistive technology to support the student's participation in written assignments. This technology allows the student to dictate their responses, and the software converts their speech into text. It can significantly enhance the student's ability to complete written tasks independently and effectively, despite their physical limitations.

QUESTION 85

Answer: B

Explanation: The most effective way to integrate affective and social skills with academic curricula is by embedding social skill development within academic lessons and activities. This approach ensures that social skills are taught in context, allowing students to practice and apply them in real-life situations. By making social skill development a natural part of the academic environment, students can better understand the relevance and importance of these skills in various contexts.

QUESTION 86

Answer: C

Explanation: The primary consideration for special education teachers when incorporating instructional and assistive technology should be to ensure that the technology aligns with students' individual needs and enhances their learning experiences. The technology chosen should be relevant, accessible, and supportive of the students' educational goals and objectives. It should facilitate their learning, engagement, and independence while addressing their specific challenges or disabilities. The focus should be on using technology as a tool to enhance and complement the teaching and learning process rather than replacing human interaction and support in the classroom.

QUESTION 87

Answer: C

Explanation: Option C is the correct answer because it suggests using a different reading assessment that includes visual aids and graphic organizers. For students with reading difficulties like Sarah, using visual aids and graphic organizers can help enhance their understanding of the text and make the assessment more accessible. This modification aligns with the principles of RTI, as it aims to provide evidence-based interventions and instruction that identify and support students at risk. Options A, B, and D do not address Sarah's specific needs and may not yield accurate data to monitor her progress effectively.

QUESTION 88

Answer: D

Explanation: Option D is the correct answer because modifying the assessment content to match Michael's instructional level will make the assessment more accessible and reduce his frustration and anxiety. RTI strategies aim to identify students at risk and provide evidence-based interventions, and modifying the assessment is an essential part of this process. Options A, B, and C address Michael's emotional state but do not directly address the need to identify his specific areas of struggle in math, which is the primary purpose of the assessment.

QUESTION 89

Answer: B

Explanation: Option B is the correct answer because using an informal writing sample where students can choose their own writing topics allows Ms. Ramirez to assess their progress in a way that aligns with the principles of RTI. Allowing students to choose their own topics reflects their interests and individual needs, providing more accurate data to identify areas of growth and areas where additional support may be necessary. Option A is not appropriate for multi-level assessments, as standardized tests may not capture individual progress effectively. Options C and D are not as suitable for assessing writing skills in this context.

QUESTION 90

Answer: D

Explanation: Option D is the correct answer because breaking the assessment into smaller segments and allowing John to take short breaks between sections will help accommodate his attention difficulties. This modification aligns with RTI principles by providing evidence-based interventions to support students at risk. Options A and C may add unnecessary pressure and stress for John, which can negatively impact his performance. Option B may help reduce distractions but does not directly address John's attention difficulties during the assessment.

QUESTION 91

Answer: B

Explanation: Option B is the correct answer because using a reading level assessment tool with a variety of reading passages and questions is the most effective way for Ms. Lee to determine her students' reading levels and identify areas of struggle. This multi-level assessment approach aligns with RTI principles, as it helps to identify students at risk and design evidence-based interventions. Options A, C, and D do not provide comprehensive data on students' reading levels and may not be as effective in targeting interventions appropriately.

QUESTION 92

Answer: C

Explanation: Option C is the correct answer because a cognitive assessment conducted by a licensed psychologist provides valuable information about Alex's cognitive abilities, strengths, and weaknesses. This assessment is essential for understanding his learning profile and making eligibility and program decisions for special education services. Options A, B, and D may provide relevant information, but a cognitive assessment is more comprehensive and directly informs the team about Alex's cognitive functioning, which is critical for planning appropriate instruction and support.

QUESTION 93

Answer: C

Explanation: Option C is the correct answer because using a progress monitoring tool that assesses Emily's reading and writing skills at regular intervals aligns with the topic's focus on planning, monitoring, and evaluating instruction. Progress monitoring helps Mr. Roberts track Emily's growth, identify areas of improvement or difficulty, and adjust his instructional strategies accordingly. Options A, B, and D may have their uses, but they do not specifically address the need for ongoing and targeted assessment of Emily's individual progress.

QUESTION 94

Answer: A

Explanation: Option A is the correct answer because considering Liam's medical history and records related to his physical disability is crucial for planning his IEP and making appropriate placement decisions. Understanding the extent of his physical disability and any associated medical needs will guide the team in providing necessary accommodations, assistive technology, and supportive services to ensure Liam's full access to the curriculum and school environment. Options B, C, and D are relevant but do not directly address Liam's specific physical needs and accessibility requirements.

QUESTION 95

Answer: C

Explanation: Option C is the correct answer because conducting one-on-one interviews allows Ms. Chang to assess her students' comprehension of the complex math concept in-depth. This approach provides an opportunity for individualized questioning and probing to understand each student's understanding, misconceptions, and thought processes. Option A may not reveal the depth of understanding, and options B and D may not capture the individual understanding of each student as effectively as one-on-one interviews.

QUESTION 96

Answer: A

Explanation: Option A is the correct answer because using Maria's performance on a standardized language assessment is essential for developing appropriate speech and language goals for her IEP. Standardized assessments provide objective and reliable data about Maria's language abilities and areas of difficulty. This information will help Mr. Rodriguez set measurable and specific goals that align with Maria's needs and monitor her progress over time. Options B, C, and D may provide useful insights, but they may not offer the comprehensive and standardized data needed to develop precise IEP goals.

QUESTION 97

Answer: B

Explanation: Option B is the correct answer because conducting a formal pre-referral intervention with evidence-based strategies is the first step in the screening and prereferral process. It allows Mrs. Smith to implement targeted interventions and monitor Alex's progress before considering a comprehensive psychoeducational assessment. This approach aligns with best practices in special education and helps determine if the student's learning difficulties can be addressed effectively through targeted support. Options A, C, and D are not the first recommended steps and may be more appropriate after the pre-referral intervention if needed.

QUESTION 98

Answer: C

Explanation: Option C is the correct answer because when reviewing referral documents, Mr. Johnson should first consider information about the specific academic and behavioral concerns that led to Emily's referral. This data will help him gain a clear understanding of the reasons for the referral and guide further assessment and decision-making processes. While options A, B, and D are relevant, they may not provide the immediate insight needed to address the concerns leading to the referral.

QUESTION 99

Answer: D

Explanation: Option D is the correct answer because the primary purpose of the eligibility determination process is to establish whether John meets the criteria for receiving special education services. This process involves reviewing assessment data and other relevant information to determine if John has a disability that affects his educational performance and requires specially designed instruction. While options A, B, and C may be important considerations in the overall planning process, they are not the primary purpose of the eligibility determination.

QUESTION 100

Answer: C

Explanation: Option C is the correct answer because the main goal of the screening process is to identify students who may need further assessment or intervention to support their learning needs. The screening process helps identify students who may be at risk or struggling academically or behaviorally and require additional support before determining eligibility for specific services like IEPs. While options A, B, and D may be important considerations in education, they are not the primary goal of the screening process.

QUESTION 101

Answer: C

Explanation: Option C is the correct answer because Ms. Davis's appropriate role in the eligibility decision-making process is to contribute her expertise and insights about the student's learning needs as a special education teacher. She can offer valuable input about the student's strengths, weaknesses, and the effectiveness of various instructional strategies and interventions. While options A, B, and D may be relevant responsibilities in other contexts, they are not the primary role of a special education teacher in the eligibility decision-making process.

QUESTION 102

Answer: D

Explanation: Since the student is non-verbal and communicates through a communication device, it is essential to use the technology that the student is comfortable with and proficient in. By using the communication device to present questions and obtain responses, Mr. Johnson ensures that the assessment is both accessible and fair for the student, avoiding bias related to their communication difficulties.

QUESTION 103

Answer: A

Explanation: For a student with ADHD, time management can be challenging. Providing extra time for completing the assessment will enable the student to work at their own pace, reducing stress and anxiety. This accommodation ensures that the student's performance is not solely hindered by time limitations and helps avoid bias in the assessment process related to the student's attention difficulties.

QUESTION 104

Answer: D

Explanation: When assessing students from diverse cultural backgrounds, language barriers can lead to biased results. By using automatic language translation for written assessments, special education teachers can ensure that language differences do not affect the students' understanding of the questions or their ability to respond accurately. This technology promotes more objective and unbiased assessments, accommodating students who may have limited proficiency in the assessment language.

QUESTION 105

Answer: B

Explanation: By assigning a scribe to draw and label the diagrams as directed by the student, Ms. Hernandez ensures that the student's fine motor difficulties do not hinder their ability to demonstrate their knowledge. This accommodation maintains the integrity of the assessment while avoiding bias related to the student's physical disability.

QUESTION 106

Answer: B

Explanation: In the IEP development process, the special education teacher plays a crucial role in providing valuable insights into the student's strengths, weaknesses, and areas of need. They contribute their expertise to formulate appropriate goals and accommodations to meet the student's individualized requirements. However, it is essential to remember that the IEP development is a collaborative effort, and the decision-making involves input from various team members, including the student and their parents/guardians.

QUESTION 107

Answer: C

Explanation: The primary focus of the transition plan within the IEP is to ensure the student's successful transition to adulthood. It involves identifying and addressing the student's post-secondary goals, which may include college, vocational training, employment, or independent living. The IEP team collaborates to develop a comprehensive plan that incorporates necessary supports, services, and activities to facilitate a smooth transition from school to adult life.

QUESTION 108

Answer: C

Explanation: The primary objective of a Behavioral Intervention Plan (BIP) is to develop an individualized plan to address and modify specific challenging behaviors exhibited by a student. It involves identifying the triggers, replacement behaviors, and appropriate interventions to support the student in learning more adaptive ways of dealing with challenging situations. A standardized BIP template may not effectively address the unique needs of each student.

QUESTION 109

Answer: B

Explanation: Parents/guardians are essential members of the IEP team and have the right to actively participate in the IEP review process. Their input, insights, and concerns about their child's progress are crucial in making informed decisions regarding the necessary modifications and supports. Collaboration between parents/guardians and the IEP team ensures that the student's needs are met effectively, and the IEP remains a truly individualized plan.

QUESTION 110

Answer: C

Explanation: General education teachers have a critical role in supporting students with IEPs in the inclusive classroom. They are responsible for modifying the curriculum to align with the student's IEP objectives and providing necessary accommodations to help the student access the content and demonstrate their learning. This ensures that the student's IEP goals are integrated into the general education setting and that they have equal access to education alongside their peers.

QUESTION 111

Answer: B

Explanation: In the assessment and program planning process, it is essential to gather comprehensive data to make informed decisions. Given the student's significant challenges, conducting further assessments, such as specific reading and writing assessments, cognitive assessments, and observations, will help in understanding the student's specific learning needs and strengths. Rushing into decisions without gathering sufficient data may lead to inappropriate programming.

QUESTION 112

Answer: D

Explanation: The appropriate order for developing an IEP is to first determine the student's present levels of performance, which serves as a foundation for setting appropriate and measurable annual goals. Based on these goals, accommodations are developed to support the student's access to the curriculum and learning environment. Finally, related services needed to support the student's educational progress are identified.

QUESTION 113

Answer: C

Explanation: Considering a student's cultural and linguistic background is critical to ensure that assessment results are not influenced by bias or misinterpretations. Different cultural or linguistic practices might impact how a student responds to assessment tasks. By being sensitive to these factors, special education teachers can ensure fair and accurate assessments that appropriately measure the student's abilities.

QUESTION 114

Answer: B

Explanation: Progress monitoring involves regularly collecting data on a student's performance to assess the effectiveness of the instructional strategies being implemented. It helps determine whether the student is making adequate progress toward their IEP goals and whether adjustments are needed in the instruction or interventions. This data-driven approach supports evidence-based decision-making to optimize the student's learning and program planning.

QUESTION 115

Answer: B

Explanation: Given the student's challenges with transitions and sensory sensitivities, the focus of the program planning should be on providing appropriate sensory breaks and accommodations during transitions. These supports will help the student manage their sensory needs and improve their overall ability to navigate the school environment successfully. While academic interventions and technology-based tools are important, addressing the immediate challenges related to sensory needs is crucial for the student's well-being and success in the inclusive setting.

QUESTION 116

Answer: B

Explanation: For a student with a visual impairment, providing printed handouts in large font size (Option A) might be helpful but may not be the most effective approach, as it still relies on visual access. Assigning a peer buddy to read aloud materials (Option C) might put unnecessary pressure on the student and might not be available all the time. Encouraging the student to sit closer to the board (Option D) could help to some extent, but it's not a comprehensive solution. The most appropriate strategy is to use a text-to-speech software (Option B), as it allows the student to access written materials audibly, promoting independence and equitable learning.

QUESTION 117

Answer: C

Explanation: While allowing students to choose their learning activities (Option A) and using a reward system (Option B) might be motivating for some students, they do not directly address the needs of students with dyslexia and dysgraphia for a structured and organized learning environment. Encouraging peer tutoring (Option D) can be beneficial but is not a modification strategy for the learning environment itself. The best modification strategy is to provide visual schedules and checklists (Option C), as these can help students with learning disabilities understand the daily routine, reduce anxiety, and improve time management and organizational skills.

QUESTION 118

Answer: C

Explanation: Assigning extra homework (Option A) could overwhelm the student and may not address the distraction issue during lessons. Seating the student near the window (Option B) might create more distractions and not necessarily improve focus. Allowing the student to use electronic devices for entertainment (Option D) could exacerbate distractions and disrupt the learning environment for others. The most appropriate strategy is to provide opportunities for movement and brain breaks during lessons (Option C). These breaks can help the student release excess energy, improve focus, and maintain engagement during the learning activities.

QUESTION 119

Answer: A

Explanation: Assigning advanced math problems (Option B) could lead to frustration and may discourage the student from engaging in math-related activities. Allowing the student to use a calculator for all math tasks (Option C) might be helpful in some instances, but it doesn't address the root of the learning disability. Removing the student from math class (Option D) would be exclusionary and not in the best interest of the student's overall education. The best approach is to reduce the complexity of math problems and assignments (Option A). This modification allows the student to work on math concepts at their own pace and gradually build their understanding without overwhelming challenges.

QUESTION 120

Answer: C

Explanation: Encouraging the student to take on a leadership role (Option A) might add additional pressure and exacerbate the anxiety. Assigning individual tasks (Option B) may not address the goal of fostering active participation in a small-group setting. Using competitive activities (Option D) could further discourage the student from participating due to fear of judgment or failure. The most effective method is to create a supportive and non-judgmental environment for sharing (Option C). This will help the student feel safe and comfortable to express their thoughts and ideas, gradually increasing their participation in the group discussions.

QUESTION 121

Answer: A

Explanation: Allowing the student to skip large-group activities (Option B) may hinder their social and academic integration and should be avoided whenever possible. Assigning a teacher's aide (Option C) could be helpful, but it may not directly address the sensory overload issue experienced during large-group events. Conducting social skills training (Option D) is valuable but may not fully alleviate the sensory challenges the student faces. The most beneficial strategy is to provide the student with noise-canceling headphones (Option A) during large-group activities. This accommodation can help reduce auditory overload and allow the student to better regulate their sensory input, making the large-group setting more manageable for them.

QUESTION 122

Answer: C

Explanation: Decreasing the reading difficulty (Option A) might hinder the student's progress and not address the root of the learning disability. Providing constant corrections (Option B) could increase frustration and negatively impact the student's motivation. Allowing the student to choose non-reading activities (Option D) may not lead to academic progress in reading. The best method to foster the student's individual academic success during reading sessions is to incorporate multi-sensory techniques, such as phonics and sight words (Option C). These techniques cater to the student's specific learning needs, improve word recognition, and build reading confidence over time.

QUESTION 123

Answer: A

Explanation: Grouping students based on their cultural similarities (Option B) may lead to unintentional segregation and hinder integration. Discouraging discussions about cultural differences (Option C) can stifle cultural awareness and appreciation. Implementing a color-blind approach (Option D) disregards the richness of cultural diversity and does not foster a sense of belonging for all students. The most effective method to facilitate students' integration and promote a sense of belonging is to organize a multicultural fair (Option A). This event allows students to share and celebrate their unique cultural backgrounds, fostering a positive and inclusive classroom environment that respects and values diversity.

QUESTION 124

Answer: C

Explanation: Providing pre-written study notes (Option A) may be helpful, but it does not directly address the student's memory deficits or teach them strategies for retention. Rote memorization techniques (Option B) can be ineffective for individuals with memory issues. Reducing the amount of information covered in each lesson (Option D) might lead to gaps in learning and does not equip the student with essential memory strategies. The most effective method is to teach mnemonic devices and memory aids (Option C). These techniques help the student encode information in a more structured and memorable way, improving their ability to recall and retain important concepts.

QUESTION 125

Answer: C

Explanation: Providing external rewards (Option A) might motivate the student initially but does not teach them to develop self-assessment skills. Assigning shorter study sessions with frequent breaks (Option B) can be helpful, but it doesn't directly address self-assessment. Allowing the student to listen to music (Option D) may or may not be beneficial, depending on individual preferences. The most effective way to teach self-assessment strategies is to use a timer and encourage the student to track their focus time (Option C). By using a timer, the student can monitor and evaluate their attention span and gradually work on extending their focus periods, leading to improved academic performance.

QUESTION 126

Answer: C

Explanation: Simplifying all instructions and content (Option A) may not adequately challenge the student or teach them cognitive strategies. Relying on others for clarifications (Option B) may not always be feasible and may hinder the student's independence. Allowing extra time (Option D) is an accommodation that can be helpful but does not directly teach cognitive strategies for comprehension. The most effective method is to teach the student to identify keywords and context clues (Option C). These strategies can help the student better grasp the main ideas and important information in written and verbal communications, improving their overall comprehension skills.

QUESTION 127

Answer: A

Explanation: Providing written transcripts (Option B) and using audio recordings (Option C) are helpful accommodations but do not directly address the need to teach learning strategies for perception and sequencing. Assigning a peer buddy (Option D) might be beneficial, but it should not be the primary method for teaching learning strategies. The most effective method is to break complex tasks into smaller, manageable steps (Option A). This approach allows the student to process and complete tasks incrementally, reducing the cognitive load and making the overall task more achievable for someone with perception and sequencing challenges.

QUESTION 128

Answer: C

Explanation: While implementing a token economy system (Option A) might be a potential intervention, it is not the first step in conducting an FBA. Interviewing the student's parents (Option B) is important but may not provide direct insights into the behaviors displayed during academic tasks. Conducting a review of the student's academic progress (Option D) is necessary but does not address the need to identify the specific triggers and consequences of the challenging behaviors. The most appropriate step to take first when conducting an FBA is to observe the student during academic tasks (Option C). This observation allows the special education teacher to gather data on antecedents (triggers) and consequences related to the challenging behaviors, helping to identify patterns and inform the development of a targeted behavioral intervention plan.

QUESTION 129

Answer: C

Explanation: Implementing a punishment system (Option A) may not address the underlying reasons for the disruptive behaviors and could lead to negative consequences. Providing additional academic support (Option B) might be helpful, but it does not directly address the need for behavior intervention. Removing the student from the classroom (Option D) might not foster inclusion and is not a positive approach to addressing disruptive behaviors. The crucial component to include in the BIP is identifying replacement behaviors and teaching appropriate social skills (Option C). By teaching the student more appropriate ways to communicate and interact with others, the BIP focuses on positive behavioral supports and helps the student develop alternative responses to their disruptive behaviors.

QUESTION 130

Answer: C

Explanation: Increasing the number of assignments (Option A) might overwhelm the student and worsen their ability to stay on task. Allowing the student to work in isolation (Option B) may not be the most effective solution, as some students with ADHD benefit from environmental cues and support. Providing rewards only if all assignments are completed (Option D) could discourage the student if they struggle to complete tasks. The effective modification to make in the BIP is using a visual timer to break the work into manageable segments (Option C). The visual timer helps the student understand the duration of each segment, promotes time management, and allows the student to see the progress they are making, increasing their ability to stay on task during independent work.

QUESTION 131

Answer: B

Explanation: While monitoring the student's academic performance (Option A) is essential, it does not directly measure the effectiveness of the BIP in addressing disruptive behaviors. Feedback from peers and teachers (Option C) can provide valuable insights but may not be objective or directly related to the success of the BIP. Tracking the student's attendance and punctuality (Option D) is not directly relevant to evaluating the BIP's effectiveness on communication and behavior. The data that should be collected to evaluate the success of the BIP is the frequency and intensity of the disruptive behaviors (Option B). This data helps assess whether the BIP is effectively reducing or managing the challenging behaviors and provides important information for making necessary adjustments to the intervention plan if needed.

QUESTION 132

Answer: D

Explanation: While job shadowing opportunities (Option A) and internships (Option C) can be valuable experiences, they might not directly cater to the student's specific interest in computer programming. Enrolling the student in a vocational training program for office administration (Option B) may not align with their career aspirations. The most effective career and vocational program to support the student's interest in computer programming is to facilitate online coding courses tailored to their specific interests (Option D). Online courses offer flexibility and can be customized to suit the student's accessibility needs, allowing them to pursue their passion in a supportive learning environment.

QUESTION 133

Answer: B

Explanation: Using standardized textbooks (Option A) may not adequately address the diverse cultural and linguistic backgrounds of the students. Focusing on one dominant cultural perspective (Option C) may lead to cultural bias and exclusion of other students' experiences. Assigning separate tasks based on cultural backgrounds (Option D) could perpetuate stereotypes and undermine the goal of inclusive education. The most effective strategy for developing instructional content is to incorporate multicultural literature and diverse perspectives in lessons (Option B). This approach fosters cultural awareness, inclusivity, and respect for students' unique identities and backgrounds.

QUESTION 134

Answer: C

Explanation: Providing extra reading practice with grade-level English texts (Option A) may overwhelm the student and hinder their language development. Using simplified reading materials (Option B) might not address the student's need to access grade-level content. Focusing solely on improving the student's reading skills in English (Option D) may not take into account their language barriers. The best approach is to incorporate bilingual resources and translated materials (Option C). This allows the student to access content in their native language while gradually developing their reading skills in English, promoting both language proficiency and academic progress.

QUESTION 135

Answer: D

Explanation: Providing lists of potential job opportunities (Option A) might not adequately prepare students for the workforce without hands-on experiences. Arranging college visits (Option B) is helpful for career exploration, but it may not align with the transition needs of all students with disabilities. Facilitating vocational training exclusively for specific disabilities (Option C) could perpetuate segregation and limit students' career options. The crucial component to include in an effective transition program is offering opportunities for community-based work experiences (Option D). These experiences allow students to gain practical skills, explore various career paths, and foster independence, increasing their readiness for post-school life.

QUESTION 136

Answer: C

Explanation: In this situation, it is essential to recognize the signs of frustration displayed by the student with autism (rocking and avoiding eye contact). Removing the student from the classroom may exacerbate their feelings of exclusion and frustration. Instead, by providing a visual schedule or agenda, the student with ASD can better understand the structure of the discussion and feel more included. Checking in with the student privately afterward allows for further support and understanding of their perspective. This strategy promotes a positive and inclusive classroom environment, fostering rapport with all students.

QUESTION 137

Answer: C

Explanation: Students with specific learning disabilities may experience test anxiety, which can hinder their performance. Offering an alternative assessment method, like an oral exam, can alleviate the pressure and provide a more conducive environment for the student to demonstrate their knowledge. Option A, providing extra time and isolation, may still contribute to anxiety and isolation. Option B, while helpful, might not be sufficient to address the root cause of the anxiety. Option D is unrelated to the assessment process and does not directly address the student's test anxiety.

QUESTION 138

Answer: D

Explanation: While options A, B, and C show consideration for the student with a hearing impairment, option D is the best way to establish rapport and create an inclusive environment for both the student with the hearing impairment and their classmates. Visual aids and demonstrations benefit all students, including those without disabilities, as they enhance understanding and engagement. By utilizing visual aids, the teacher promotes an inclusive learning experience where all students can participate effectively.

QUESTION 139

Answer: C

Explanation: Option C is the most effective way to address the situation and maintain rapport with the entire class. Implementing a hand-raising rule for all students sets clear expectations for classroom behavior. This strategy creates consistency and fairness, and it helps manage disruptions from the student with ADHD without singling them out. Additionally, acknowledging and redirecting positive behaviors of the student with ADHD can be very encouraging, reinforcing their engagement and participation. Options A and B could be considered as part of a broader behavior management plan but should be implemented in a positive and supportive manner, not as a punitive measure. Option D, isolating the student, is not an inclusive approach and may further alienate the student with ADHD from their peers.

QUESTION 140

Answer: B

Explanation: Option B is the most effective strategy in this case. Creating a behavior intervention plan tailored to the student's needs and incorporating positive reinforcement for appropriate behaviors can help manage their emotional and aggressive reactions. This approach focuses on teaching and reinforcing positive alternatives to aggression, helping the student develop coping skills and self-regulation. Options A, C, and D do not address the underlying behavioral challenges and may isolate the student or limit their learning opportunities.

QUESTION 141

Answer: B

Explanation: Option B is the most suitable strategy in this situation. Providing the student with noise-canceling headphones can help reduce auditory sensory overload, while having a quiet corner allows them to take breaks when needed. These environmental modifications enable the student to self-regulate and manage sensory challenges effectively. Option A would overly restrict the student's access to learning opportunities, and Option C might lead to increased feelings of exclusion. Option D, while beneficial, is not the most efficient strategy for addressing sensory overload.

QUESTION 142

Answer: C

Explanation: Option C is the most appropriate crisis prevention strategy in this case. Gradual desensitization involves systematically introducing the student to the challenging task in manageable steps, helping them build confidence and tolerance over time. Providing emotional support during the process helps the student feel understood and supported. Option A could exacerbate frustration, Option B may lead to missed learning opportunities, and Option D does not address the underlying issue or promote growth.

QUESTION 143

Answer: D

Explanation: Option D is the most effective strategy for managing impulsive behaviors in group activities. Clear rules and visual cues for turn-taking help the student with ADHD understand the expectations and structure of the activity, promoting better impulse control. This approach benefits the entire group and creates an inclusive and supportive learning environment. Options A and C isolate the student and do not address the root cause of the impulsive behaviors. Option B, while well-intentioned, might not be sufficient in helping the student develop appropriate social skills in a group setting.

QUESTION 144

Answer: C

Explanation: Option C is the most effective strategy in this situation. Graphic organizers and concept maps help students with learning disabilities to organize information visually, identify key concepts, and understand the relationships between different ideas in complex texts. This approach supports reading comprehension and encourages recognition of relationships across disciplines. Options A and B might limit the student's exposure to challenging texts and impede their growth. Option D, while well-intentioned, does not address the specific issue of comprehension difficulty.

QUESTION 145

Answer: B

Explanation: Option B is the most effective strategy in this case. Providing hands-on science experiments allows the student to experience abstract concepts in a concrete and tangible way. This approach enhances their understanding and retention of scientific principles while encouraging maintenance and generalization of academic skills. Options A and D may not fully address the student's specific learning needs and interests. Option C could potentially limit the student's overall educational experience.

QUESTION 146

Answer: C

Explanation: Option C is the most effective strategy for teaching essential vocabulary and content to ELLs while accommodating their language needs. Visual aids, realia (real-life objects), and context-rich examples provide additional support and help make the content more understandable and relatable. This approach promotes language development alongside content learning, fostering an inclusive and supportive classroom environment. Options A and B segregate and limit ELLs' opportunities for academic growth. Option D, while potentially beneficial, does not address the broader issue of making content accessible to ELLs.

QUESTION 147

Answer: C

Explanation: Option C is the most effective strategy to promote interdisciplinary learning and help students recognize relationships across disciplines. Allowing students to explore connections between different subjects through projects and real-life applications fosters critical thinking, creativity, and a deeper understanding of how knowledge is interconnected. This approach enhances engagement and accommodates diverse learning styles. Options A and B limit students' exposure to interdisciplinary learning experiences and may hinder their ability to see the broader connections between subjects. Option D segregates students based on their abilities, which goes against the principles of inclusive education.

QUESTION 148

Answer: C

Explanation: Option C is the most effective strategy in this situation. Role-playing exercises provide an opportunity for the students to observe and practice problem-solving and conflict-resolution skills in a controlled and supportive environment. By modeling appropriate behavior and guiding the students through different scenarios, they can develop essential social skills and strategies to resolve conflicts constructively. Options A and D do not address the core issue and may limit the students' social interactions. Option B, while helpful, might not be as effective as interactive role-playing exercises for teaching practical social skills.

QUESTION 149

Answer: C

Explanation: Option C is the most effective strategy to teach appropriate expectations for personal and social behavior. A behavior plan that explicitly outlines expected behaviors and provides positive reinforcement for compliance helps the student understand clear expectations and encourages them to engage in positive behaviors. This approach focuses on positive behavior supports and promotes self-regulation skills. Options A and D isolate the student and do not address the need for explicit guidance and reinforcement. Option B may be counterproductive and might exacerbate the student's challenging behaviors.

QUESTION 150

Answer: C

Explanation: Option C is the most effective strategy in this case. Providing structured group activities with petitions helps students with learning disabilities and attention issues understand their responsibilities and contributions to the project. This approach encourages problem-solving, cooperation, and effective communication within the group. Options A and D limit the students' opportunities for collaboration and may not foster essential social skills. Option B, while promoting social connections, might not address the challenges these students face during group work.

QUESTION 151

Answer: A

Explanation: Option A is the most effective strategy for teaching self-regulation and conflict-resolution skills in overwhelming situations. Providing a sensory break area allows the student to recognize their feelings of sensory overload and proactively take steps to calm down. This approach fosters self-awareness and teaches the student to cope with overwhelming environments constructively. Options B and C do not provide the student with opportunities to learn and practice self-regulation skills. Option D is not directly related to teaching self-regulation and conflict-resolution skills in overwhelming situations.

QUESTION 152

Answer: B

Explanation: Option B is the most effective strategy for promoting a successful transition for the student with ASD. Visiting the postsecondary education facility beforehand allows the student to familiarize themselves with the new environment, routines, and expectations. This can help reduce anxiety and increase the student's comfort level during the actual transition. Option A provides a schedule, but without the context of visiting the facility, it may not be as meaningful for the student. Option C, advising the student to avoid thinking about the changes, may not address their legitimate concerns and might lead to avoidance behaviors. Option D, while helpful, might not fully address the student's personal concerns and anxieties.

QUESTION 153

Answer: A

Explanation: Option A is the most effective strategy for promoting a successful transition for the student with a learning disability. Introducing the student to the new teachers and classmates before the transition allows them to establish relationships and become familiar with the new academic environment. This approach helps alleviate anxiety and fosters a sense of belonging and support. Option B might be overwhelming for the student and may not address the social aspect of the transition. Option C could increase stress for the student and might not be necessary for a successful transition. Option D, while important, may not directly address the student's concerns about coping with new academic expectations.

QUESTION 154

Answer: B

Explanation: Option B is the most effective strategy for promoting a successful transition to employment for the student with intellectual disabilities. Providing the student with trial work experiences allows them to explore different job settings, identify their interests, and build valuable vocational skills. This hands-on approach can increase their confidence and help them make informed decisions about future employment opportunities. Option A might not be as relevant for students with intellectual disabilities as for other job seekers. Option C might be considered later on, but immediate employment experiences are valuable for skill development. Option D, providing a list of job openings, may not fully support the student's exploration and preparation for employment.

QUESTION 155

Answer: A

Explanation: Option A is the most effective strategy for promoting a successful transition for the student with ADHD. Providing detailed organizational tools and time management resources can help the student stay on top of assignments and manage their multiple classrooms effectively. These tools may include planners, calendars, and reminders to support their executive functioning skills. Option B, while beneficial, might not be feasible in all settings and may not empower the student to develop self-regulation skills. Option C, segregating the student, may not be the most inclusive approach, and it may not prepare them for future academic settings. Option D, relying on memory and instincts, might not be sufficient for a smooth transition and academic success.

QUESTION 156

Answer: D

Explanation: For a student with ADHD, providing visual aids and incorporating hands-on activities can be highly beneficial. These strategies help to capture the student's interest, maintain focus, and enhance their understanding of the material. The use of visuals aids and interactive experiences cater to different learning styles, making it easier for the student to stay engaged and attentive during lessons.

QUESTION 157

Answer: C

Explanation: Students with disabilities have diverse needs, and a "one-size-fits-all" approach to behavioral expectations may not be effective. It is crucial to consider each student's individual abilities and challenges when establishing behavioral expectations. Tailoring expectations allows for reasonable and achievable goals, fostering a positive learning environment that promotes growth and success for each student.

QUESTION 158

Answer: C

Explanation: For a student with autism spectrum disorder (ASD), maintaining a consistent daily routine is crucial to reduce anxiety and improve their overall classroom experience. However, the real world can involve unexpected changes. The best approach is to gradually introduce changes in the routine and provide advance notice to prepare the student for the upcoming modifications. Visual schedules can also be immensely helpful, as they offer a clear and predictable representation of the daily schedule, helping the student understand what to expect and reducing anxiety related to changes.

QUESTION 159

Answer: C

Explanation: Breaking tasks into smaller, manageable steps is an effective strategy for promoting independence in students with disabilities. By dividing complex tasks into achievable components, students are more likely to succeed and feel a sense of accomplishment. Positive reinforcement for completing these smaller steps further encourages students to take responsibility for their learning and motivates them to tackle more challenging tasks. Avoiding difficult tasks (option b) and providing constant support (option a) can hinder the development of independence and self-reliance in students.

QUESTION 160

Answer: C

Explanation: For a student with dyslexia, a multi-sensory approach to reading instruction, like the Orton-Gillingham method, is highly effective. This approach engages multiple senses (visual, auditory, kinesthetic) to reinforce learning and supports the development of reading skills. By incorporating activities that involve seeing, hearing, and touching, the student's reading comprehension and overall literacy can significantly improve.

QUESTION 161

Answer: C

Explanation: Differentiation involves tailoring instruction to cater to the unique strengths, interests, and learning styles of each student. This approach ensures that all students, including those with disabilities or exceptional abilities, receive appropriate and effective instruction. By adapting teaching methods, materials, and assessments, teachers can create an inclusive learning environment that supports the success of all students.

QUESTION 162

Answer: D

Explanation: For a student with ADHD, incorporating active learning strategies and interactive discussions during lectures can significantly enhance engagement and focus. Passive listening may be challenging for the student, but involving them in discussions, group activities, and hands-on experiences promotes better attention and understanding of the material. It encourages active participation, which is conducive to learning for students with attention difficulties.

QUESTION 163

Answer: C

Explanation: The effective use of technology in the classroom involves integrating it purposefully to support and enhance the learning process. When technology aligns with instructional goals, it can provide interactive, adaptive, and personalized learning experiences for students. Utilizing technology strategically as a tool to aid learning can cater to different learning styles and help students achieve success in the general curriculum.

QUESTION 164

Answer: C

Explanation: In an inclusive classroom, embracing cultural diversity is essential for promoting a positive and enriching learning environment. By incorporating diverse perspectives, experiences, and materials into the curriculum, teachers can foster respect, understanding, and appreciation for different cultures among students. This approach enhances students' learning by making connections between their own experiences and those of others, promoting empathy and critical thinking.

QUESTION 165

Answer: B

Explanation: For students with autism who have challenges with verbal communication, the Picture Exchange Communication System (PECS) is an evidence-based strategy. PECS uses pictures or symbols to enable students to communicate their needs, wants, and thoughts. This system promotes language development, independence, and social interactions. By using visual supports, the student can better understand and communicate with others, reducing frustration and improving communication skills.

QUESTION 166

Answer: C

Explanation: A functional behavior assessment (FBA) is a critical step in developing effective behavioral interventions. By identifying the functions and triggers of a student's challenging behavior, educators can design targeted interventions that address the root causes rather than simply reacting to the behavior. This proactive approach allows for the creation of individualized and positive behavior support plans that are more likely to bring about lasting behavioral improvements.

QUESTION 167

Answer: A

Explanation: A behavior contract is a positive and proactive intervention that sets clear expectations for the student's behavior. By rewarding the student for refraining from interrupting and offering incentives for appropriate behavior, the contract reinforces positive actions. This approach focuses on encouraging desired behavior rather than solely relying on punishment. It helps the student become more aware of their actions and encourages self-regulation, leading to a reduction in disruptive behaviors over time.

QUESTION 168

Answer: C

Explanation: Social narratives and role-playing activities provide structured opportunities for students to practice and develop social skills in a controlled and supportive environment. Through social narratives, students can learn appropriate social behaviors and responses to various situations. Role-playing allows them to practice these skills with guidance and feedback from teachers and peers. These interventions help students with disabilities build social competence and confidence in their interactions with others.

QUESTION 169

Answer: C

Explanation: Generalization of communication and social skills involves applying these skills in different environments and with various individuals. Collaborating with parents and caregivers is crucial in supporting the transfer of these skills beyond the classroom. When parents and caregivers reinforce and practice these skills at home and in other community settings, students have more opportunities to generalize their abilities. This collaboration ensures that students can effectively use their communication and social skills in a range of real-life situations.

QUESTION 170

Answer: C

Explanation: For students with intellectual disabilities transitioning to adulthood, a comprehensive transition plan is essential. This plan should include vocational training and community-based experiences to develop functional living skills and job-related abilities. By providing opportunities to gain real-world experience, such as internships or job-shadowing, the student can explore different career options and build essential skills needed for independent living and meaningful employment.

QUESTION 171

Answer: C

Explanation: Teaching functional living skills in meaningful contexts allows students to see the relevance and practicality of these skills in their daily lives. By using real-life scenarios and incorporating the skills into activities that align with the students' interests and goals, learning becomes more engaging and applicable. This approach promotes better retention and transfer of skills to real-world situations.

QUESTION 172

Answer: B

Explanation: For students with autism who may benefit from visual supports and clear routines, providing visual schedules and step-by-step instructions is highly effective. Visual supports help the student understand the sequence of tasks and can serve as reminders for each step. This approach promotes independence by guiding the student through the tasks and enables them to develop their daily living skills at their own pace.

QUESTION 173

Answer: C

Explanation: When preparing students for post-secondary education or employment, it is essential to identify and build on their strengths and talents. Focusing on these positive aspects empowers students, builds their self-confidence, and provides a solid foundation for future success. Recognizing and utilizing their strengths allows students to make meaningful contributions and find areas of interest in their chosen fields.

QUESTION 174

Answer: C

Explanation: Community integration is crucial for students with disabilities to develop social skills, independence, and a sense of belonging. Actively participating in community activities allows them to engage with their surroundings, build relationships, and practice functional living skills in real-life settings. By providing opportunities for community integration, students can learn to navigate the world around them and become more confident and independent individuals.

QUESTION 175

Answer: D

Explanation: Cooperative learning activities that involve diverse groups of students encourage collaboration, empathy, and understanding. By working together, students can learn from one another's unique perspectives and experiences, fostering respect for diversity and positive interactions among all students. It helps create an inclusive environment where students feel valued and appreciated for their contributions, regardless of their cultural backgrounds or abilities.

QUESTION 176

Answer: B

Explanation: Research consistently supports the effectiveness of phonics instruction, especially for students with reading disabilities. Phonics helps students understand the relationship between letters and their corresponding sounds, enabling them to decode words accurately. This approach builds a strong foundation for reading and improves overall reading skills.

QUESTION 177

Answer: C

Explanation: Visual supports, like picture cards and communication boards, are valuable tools for fostering communication skills in students with disabilities and those with different linguistic backgrounds or using alternative and augmentative communication systems. These visual aids provide additional context, aid comprehension, and help students express their thoughts and needs effectively. Visual supports can be adapted to cater to individual students' preferences and can create a more inclusive and cohesive classroom environment.

QUESTION 178

Answer: B

Explanation: In a special education context, hands-on instruction with step-by-step demonstrations is highly effective for teaching daily living skills. Students with diverse abilities may benefit from direct modeling and guided practice to learn essential tasks. By demonstrating the skills and then providing supervised practice, Mr. Davis can offer individualized support and adapt the teaching approach to meet each student's needs.

QUESTION 179

Answer: B

Explanation: Rearranging the desks to create a U-shaped seating arrangement will allow the student with physical disabilities to easily navigate the classroom using their wheelchair. This setup provides enough space for the student to move around and participate in classroom activities without facing barriers posed by rows of desks. Installing a ramp (option a) is essential for overall accessibility, but it may not directly address the issue of the classroom's seating arrangement. Providing a separate study area outside the classroom (option c) may isolate the student and limit their inclusion in classroom activities. Assigning a peer buddy (option d) might be helpful but should not be the primary adaptation for addressing physical barriers in the classroom.

QUESTION 180

Answer: C

Explanation: For a student with autism and sensory sensitivities, creating a sensory break area with dimmed lighting and noise-cancelling headphones can be a helpful adaptation. This designated area allows the student to take breaks when feeling overwhelmed and regulate their sensory input. Brighter lights (option a) would likely exacerbate the student's sensory issues. While background music (option b) might work for some students, it could be distracting or distressing for others with sensory sensitivities. Assigning a classroom aide (option d) may be unnecessary and may not directly address the physical environment's impact on the student's sensory experiences.

QUESTION 181

Answer: D

Explanation: The most appropriate adaptation for a student with a visual impairment is to use a digital whiteboard with screen-reader compatibility (option d). This way, the student can access the information presented on the whiteboard using assistive technology like a screen reader. Providing a magnifying glass (option a) might not be sufficient for clear and accessible information. Using a larger font (option b) on the whiteboard might help to some extent, but it may not be as effective as the digital whiteboard with screen-reader compatibility. While an audio recording (option c) could be useful for some scenarios, it might not be as interactive or real-time as the digital whiteboard with screen-reader compatibility.

QUESTION 182

Answer: A

Explanation: To provide optimal learning opportunities for a student with dyslexia, using text-to-speech software to read the materials aloud (option a) can be extremely beneficial. This adaptation supports the student in accessing written information without relying on their reading skills, making the content more accessible. While a peer tutor (option b) might help, the text-to-speech software offers independence and immediate access to information. Using a different font style (option c) might not be sufficient to address the reading challenges for students with dyslexia. Providing larger textbooks with simplified language (option d) might not address the core issue of reading difficulties and may lead to a disconnect with the standard curriculum.

QUESTION 183

Answer: B

Explanation: To provide optimal learning opportunities for a student with ADHD, providing additional breaks during longer classroom activities (option b) can be helpful. These breaks allow the student to refocus, regulate their energy, and reduce restlessness, which may lead to increased engagement during the activities. Increasing the duration of classroom activities gradually (option a) may overwhelm the student with ADHD. Seating the student near the front of the classroom (option c) might not be sufficient to address attention difficulties and could still expose the student to distractions. Assigning the student to lead group activities (option d) might add more pressure and responsibilities, potentially increasing their anxiety and impacting their focus during the activities.

QUESTION 184

Answer: B

Explanation: For students with dyscalculia, research has shown that using hands-on manipulatives (option b) can be highly effective in helping them understand math concepts. Manipulatives allow the student to visualize and interact with the mathematical concepts, making abstract ideas more concrete and accessible. Implementing timed quizzes (option a) can increase anxiety and hinder the student's understanding of math. Assigning advanced math problems (option c) might overwhelm the student and not address their specific learning needs. Using complex mathematical language (option d) can further complicate understanding and hinder the student's ability to grasp essential concepts.

QUESTION 185

Answer: A

Explanation: Research supports providing breaks (option a) for students with ADHD to release excess energy and refocus during lessons. Short breaks can help the student stay on task and prevent restlessness. Assigning extra math problems (option b) might overwhelm the student and lead to increased frustration. Using abstract visuals and diagrams (option c) might be beneficial for some students but might not address the specific focus and attention challenges faced by students with ADHD. Encouraging parallel activities (option d) could lead to distraction and reduced comprehension of the math content.

QUESTION 186

Answer: C

Explanation: For students with visual impairments, research supports using tactile graphics and braille materials (option c) to make math concepts accessible. Tactile graphics allow the student to feel and explore visual representations of mathematical information, enabling a deeper understanding. Audio recordings (option a) may not provide sufficient access to visual information. A sighted guide (option b) might be helpful but could be impractical for constant support during math lessons. Increasing font size (option d) may not be applicable to tactile learning needs.

QUESTION 187

Answer: B

Explanation: Research supports the use of real-life examples (option b) to help students with learning disabilities in mathematics grasp abstract concepts. By relating math to practical situations, students can better understand how abstract concepts apply to real-world scenarios. Reducing assignments (option a) might not address the core issue of understanding abstract concepts. Memorization techniques (option c) might not facilitate true comprehension and can add more stress. Encouraging competition (option d) could increase anxiety and hinder the student's learning process.

QUESTION 188

Answer: B

Explanation: Research supports the use of songs and rhymes (option b) to teach counting and number sequencing for students with intellectual disabilities. Music and rhythm can aid memory and help make abstract concepts more engaging and accessible. Engaging the student in complex problem-solving tasks (option a) may overwhelm the student and not address their foundational number sense needs. Providing pre-written solutions (option c) may hinder the student's learning process and reduce critical thinking. Assigning additional homework (option d) might not be as effective as using interactive and engaging methods like songs and rhymes.

QUESTION 189

Answer: C

Explanation: Teaching the student emotional regulation techniques and conflict resolution skills (option c) is the most effective strategy for fostering their social skills and self-management. By equipping the student with these essential skills, they can better handle their anger and conflicts with peers, leading to more positive social interactions. Isolating the student during conflicts (option a) may not address the underlying issues and can lead to further social isolation. Implementing a behavior chart with public rewards (option b) might not target the specific social skill deficits and may not be effective in addressing emotional and behavioral challenges. Assigning a peer mentor (option d) might provide some support, but it is essential to empower the student to develop their self-management and social skills.

QUESTION 190

Answer: C

Explanation: Encouraging the student to set achievable goals and celebrate progress (option c) is the most effective strategy for increasing their self-esteem and self-awareness. By setting realistic goals and acknowledging their accomplishments, the student can develop a sense of self-efficacy and build a positive self-perception. Constant praise and rewards (option a) may feel insincere and might not address the student's feelings of inadequacy. Providing accommodations (option b) can be helpful, but it may not directly impact the student's self-esteem. Assigning the student to a remedial class (option d) might be perceived negatively and could further affect their self-esteem.

QUESTION 191

Answer: B

Explanation: Implementing a visual schedule and communication cards (option b) is the most effective strategy for developing self-advocacy skills in the student with autism. These tools can help the student communicate their needs and preferences independently, promoting self-determination. Assigning a teacher's aide (option a) to anticipate the student's needs might not encourage self-advocacy and could create dependency. Limiting responsibilities (option c) may hinder the student's growth in self-determination. Encouraging peers to speak on the student's behalf (option d) might not support the development of self-advocacy skills and could potentially lead to misunderstandings.

QUESTION 192

Answer: D

Explanation: Providing information about inclusive extracurricular opportunities and offering support (option d) is the most effective strategy for fostering self-determination in students with disabilities. By presenting the students with available options and assuring them of support, they can make informed choices and explore activities that interest them. Exempting the students from activities (option a) can limit their opportunities for growth and social engagement. Organizing disability-specific groups (option b) might segregate the students and may not align with inclusive principles. Holding meetings with parents (option c) is essential for collaboration but should not deter students from exploring extracurricular activities.

QUESTION 193

Answer: D

Explanation: Conducting regular meetings with the student to discuss their goals and concerns (option d) is the most effective strategy for fostering self-advocacy and self-determination in the student with a physical disability. Engaging the student in discussions about their aspirations, barriers they face, and their opinions on decision-making empowers them to take an active role in their education. Assigning a personal aide (option a) might hinder the development of self-advocacy skills. Advocating for accessibility modifications (option b) is essential, but it should complement efforts to involve the student in decision-making. Discouraging the student from participating (option c) can undermine their confidence and autonomy.

QUESTION 194

Answer: D

Explanation: Encouraging the students to attend workshops and career fairs (option d) is the most effective strategy for promoting vocational/career competence. These events provide students with disabilities the opportunity to explore various industries, gain insights into potential careers, and make informed decisions about their vocational aspirations. Vocational assessments (option a) are valuable tools, but they should be complemented by hands-on experiences. Assigning students to volunteer (option b) might be beneficial, but attending workshops and career fairs offers a broader exposure to different career options. Focusing solely on academic subjects (option c) might neglect the practical skills and experiences necessary for vocational competence.

QUESTION 195

Answer: B

Explanation: Collaborating with community organizations to provide inclusive recreational opportunities (option b) is the most effective strategy for promoting the student's participation in community leisure activities. Inclusive programs foster social inclusion and allow the student to interact with peers without disabilities, enhancing their overall recreational experiences. Organizing a special leisure program (option a) might further segregate the student and limit their social interactions. Discouraging the student from participating (option c) can hinder their social development and enjoyment. Providing leisure activities within the school setting (option d) may not offer the same level of community engagement and experiences.

QUESTION 196

Answer: A

Explanation: Providing the student with a specialized computer lab with assistive technology (option a) is the most effective strategy for teaching technology skills and promoting their vocational competence. This approach offers the necessary accommodations to enable the student to access technology comfortably and develop their skills in pursuing a career in technology. Exempting the student from technology-related tasks (option b) can hinder their learning and growth in this field. Offering online tutorials and resources (option c) can be beneficial but should be combined with personalized support and accommodations. Encouraging the student to pursue a different vocational interest (option d) would not be appropriate and could limit their career choices based on their disability.

QUESTION 197

Answer: b) Providing written instructions and visual aids to support task completion.

Explanation: Providing written instructions and visual aids (option b) is the most effective strategy for teaching vocational skills to students with autism. Visual supports can help compensate for challenges in social communication and support their memory and attention to detail, facilitating task completion. Assigning group projects (option a) might create stress and hinder their ability to focus on vocational skills. Neglecting social communication training (option c) could limit their vocational success in real-world job settings. Assigning a vocational coach (option d) might provide some support but should not replace efforts to enhance their independence through visual supports.

QUESTION 198

Answer: B

Explanation: Providing the student with internship opportunities (option b) at local environmental organizations is the most effective strategy for promoting their vocational competence in environmental conservation. Internships offer hands-on experiences, networking opportunities, and real-world exposure to the field, allowing the student to gain practical skills and knowledge. Discouraging the student (option a) can crush their passion and aspirations. Limiting involvement to theoretical learning (option c) might not be sufficient for vocational competence. Assigning unrelated tasks (option d) would not align with the student's career interests and potential.

QUESTION 199

Answer: C

Explanation: The Individuals with Disabilities Education Act (IDEA) was enacted in 1975 and has been reauthorized several times since then. It guarantees that all students with disabilities have the right to a free appropriate public education (FAPE) tailored to their individual needs. IDEA also mandates that students with disabilities are educated in the least restrictive environment (LRE) to the maximum extent possible, meaning they should be placed in regular education classrooms with appropriate support, services, and accommodations, unless it is demonstrated that their needs cannot be met there.

QUESTION 200

Answer: B

Explanation: In an IEP, it is essential to focus on addressing the student's specific needs related to their disability. In Tim's case, since he has difficulties with social interactions and engages in repetitive behaviors due to autism, the most appropriate goal would be to target those challenges. Reducing repetitive behaviors by 50% within six months is a specific, measurable, and time-bound goal that directly addresses one of Tim's core areas of difficulty.

QUESTION 201

Answer: B

Explanation: In 1972, the court case Mills v. Board of Education of the District of Columbia brought attention to the denial of special education services to students with disabilities. The case asserted that denying access to education due to disabilities violated the students' constitutional rights. The landmark decision emphasized that students with disabilities have the right to a free appropriate public education (FAPE) and that it should be provided in the least restrictive environment (LRE).

QUESTION 202

Answer: D

Explanation: Beneficence is an ethical principle that requires special education teachers to act in the best interests of the students with disabilities they serve. It involves promoting their well-being, ensuring their safety, and striving to enhance their learning and development. Prioritizing beneficence means making decisions and taking actions that aim to maximize the benefits for the students and improve their overall quality of life.

QUESTION 203

Answer: C

Explanation: The annual review meeting is an essential opportunity to assess the student's progress and update the IEP accordingly. Since the student is making significant progress but continues to struggle with reading comprehension, it is important for Mr. Rodriguez to address this area of need. Developing new IEP goals that specifically target reading comprehension improvement will allow the student to receive targeted support and intervention in this particular area while maintaining the progress made in other areas.

QUESTION 204

Answer: B

Explanation: Collaboration between special education teachers and general education teachers is crucial for supporting students with disabilities in inclusive classrooms. Regular meetings allow for ongoing communication, sharing of progress, and discussing any necessary adjustments to accommodations or teaching strategies. By maintaining open lines of communication and collaboration, both teachers can work together to provide the most effective learning opportunities for the student with a learning disability.

QUESTION 205

Answer: C

Explanation: For a student with multiple disabilities, communication among related services providers and school staff members needs to be efficient, consistent, and detailed. Utilizing a secure online platform allows for the sharing of comprehensive information about the student's needs, progress, and any changes in accommodations or strategies. Regular updates through this platform ensure that all relevant team members are informed and can coordinate their efforts effectively.

QUESTION 206

Answer: B

Explanation: Collaboration and communication are essential when working with teaching aides and paraprofessionals. Conducting regular team meetings allows for sharing important information, discussing effective strategies, addressing concerns, and providing professional development opportunities. It fosters a cohesive and supportive team environment, enhancing the effectiveness of support provided to students with disabilities.

QUESTION 207

Answer: C

Explanation: Collaboration with community agencies is crucial for providing meaningful learning opportunities for students with disabilities after graduation. By establishing ongoing partnerships, special education teachers can work with community representatives to develop personalized transition plans that align with each student's strengths, interests, and post-graduation goals. This collaborative approach ensures that the students receive tailored support and opportunities for successful post-school outcomes.

QUESTION 208

Answer: C

Explanation: Supporting a student with difficulties in self-regulation requires a collaborative and consistent approach from all school staff members involved in the student's education. By working together to develop a behavior management plan tailored to the student's needs, staff members can implement consistent strategies to support the student's emotional regulation. Regular progress updates and ongoing communication ensure that all staff members are informed and can provide effective support throughout the school year.

QUESTION 209

Answer: B

Explanation: The correct approach for Ms. Johnson is to conduct individualized assessments for each student showing academic challenges and consider cultural and linguistic factors. Overrepresentation of students from diverse backgrounds in special education programs may be influenced by cultural bias, language barriers, and other socio-cultural factors. Therefore, it is crucial to consider these factors during the assessment process to ensure appropriate identification and support for students with disabilities.

QUESTION 210

Answer: D

Explanation: The Civil Rights Act of 1964 was a landmark legislation that had a substantial impact on special education. It prohibited discrimination based on race, color, religion, sex, or national origin. This act led to significant changes in the education system and paved the way for equal access to education, including special education services, for all students, regardless of their background.

QUESTION 211

Answer: A

Explanation: Advances in technology have significantly impacted the identification process of students with disabilities. With the development of various assessment tools, assistive technologies, and data analytics, educators can better identify and diagnose students' specific learning needs and disabilities. Technology plays a crucial role in conducting more accurate and comprehensive assessments, leading to more tailored support and interventions for students. Options B, C, and D are not directly linked to advances in technology. They are more influenced by social, cultural, and educational policies and practices.

QUESTION 212

Answer: C

Explanation: Universal Design for Learning (UDL) is a research-based approach that promotes inclusive education by offering multiple means of representation, engagement, and expression to meet the diverse needs of all learners, including students with disabilities. It focuses on creating flexible learning environments and providing various tools and resources to support students in accessing the curriculum and demonstrating their understanding in different ways. Options A and B are not conducive to fostering an inclusive learning environment, as they involve either placing students with disabilities in general education classrooms without additional support or segregating them in separate classrooms. Option D is not a best practice, as standardized teaching methods may not address the individualized needs of students with disabilities.

QUESTION 213

Answer: D

Explanation: Mr. Lee's belief in the importance of early intervention is supported by research and evidence that early identification and intervention for children with developmental delays or disabilities can significantly improve their developmental outcomes and academic success. By providing targeted support and services at an early age, children can make significant progress and have a better chance of reaching their full potential. Options A, B, and C are not the primary rationale behind Mr. Lee's belief in early intervention. While early intervention may indirectly address some of these aspects, the main focus and benefit lie in improving the developmental and educational outcomes of the children.

QUESTION 214

Answer: B

Explanation: Joining a local special education teacher association and actively participating in their monthly meetings would be the most effective way for Sarah to enhance her professional skills and engage in lifelong professional growth. These associations often provide valuable resources, research-based information, and opportunities to network with other professionals in the field. Attending meetings and events focused on special education topics would help her stay updated with the latest research and best practices relevant to her profession.

QUESTION 215

Answer: B

Explanation: A peer-reviewed journal specializing in special education research would be the most beneficial resource for a special education teacher seeking up-to-date and reliable information. These journals publish articles that have undergone rigorous evaluation by experts in the field, ensuring the quality and accuracy of the research presented. By reading peer-reviewed articles, teachers can access evidence-based practices and stay informed about the latest trends in special education. Option A may provide some general teaching strategies but may not focus specifically on special education, which is what the teacher needs. Option C is not directly related to special education and may not offer the specific information required for maintaining professional standards. Option D, while promoting themes of diversity and inclusion, is not a professional resource specifically tailored to the needs of a special education teacher.

QUESTION 216

Answer: B

Explanation: Enrolling in a year-long online course covering various topics in special education would be the most effective approach to professional development for special education teachers. This comprehensive and extended course would allow teachers to delve deeper into various relevant subjects and gain a more comprehensive understanding of the field. The extended duration would provide ample time for in-depth learning, application, and reflection. Option A may provide some useful insights, but it is a one-time event and may not cover as much content as a year-long course. Option C is a brief online webinar that may offer valuable information, but its limited duration may not be sufficient for substantial professional growth. Option D, while watching educational videos can be beneficial, it lacks the structured approach and comprehensive content that a formal online course would offer.

QUESTION 217

Answer: C

Explanation: Joining a specialized professional learning community for special educators offers the best platform for collaboration and sharing best practices. These communities are designed explicitly for professionals in the field of special education, allowing teachers to connect with colleagues who have similar interests, challenges, and expertise. It provides a focused and supportive environment for discussing relevant topics, seeking advice, and sharing effective teaching strategies. Option A is a social gathering with colleagues from various professions, which may not provide the focused environment needed for meaningful collaboration. Option B, participating in an online forum open to the general public, may not be specialized enough to address the unique needs and concerns of special education teachers. Option D involves volunteering for community events unrelated to education and would not be directly relevant to professional collaboration and sharing of best practices in special education.

QUESTION 218

Answer: D

Explanation: Enrolling in a series of self-paced online courses on special education topics would be the most beneficial resource for self-paced, continuous learning. These courses offer flexibility, allowing teachers to progress at their own pace and explore a variety of relevant topics in special education in-depth. Option A, attending an annual national conference, can provide valuable insights, but it is not a continuous, self-paced resource for learning. Option B, subscribing to a monthly online magazine, can offer periodic information, but it may not provide the depth and continuity of learning that a series of courses would. Option C, joining a weekly book club focused on general education literature, is not specialized enough to support continuous learning in the field of special education.

QUESTION 219

Answer: A

Explanation: In this case, the teacher should collaborate with the school's behavior specialist to design a new behavior intervention plan that addresses Sarah's sensory processing difficulties. As a special education teacher, seeking guidance from other professionals with expertise in behavior management, particularly related to sensory issues, can provide more effective strategies to support Sarah's needs.

QUESTION 220

Answer: D

Explanation: FERPA protects the confidentiality of students' educational records. Discussing a student's behavioral challenges in a public forum, such as a professional development workshop, can potentially reveal the identity of the student and is considered a breach of confidentiality. Options A, B, and C are not violations of student confidentiality as they involve legitimate disclosures to appropriate stakeholders involved in the student's education.

QUESTION 221

Answer: A

Explanation: Providing the student with a summary of the reading passage before the assessment is an appropriate accommodation for a student with a specific learning disability in reading comprehension. It helps the student focus on the main points of the passage, which can enhance their understanding during the assessment. Options B and C are common accommodations but may not directly address the student's reading comprehension difficulty. Option D (reading the entire assessment aloud) is not appropriate as it would alter the nature of the assessment and test the student's listening comprehension rather than their reading comprehension.

QUESTION 222

Answer: C

Explanation: For a student with ADHD and impulsive behaviors like James, modifying the classroom environment can be an effective strategy. By incorporating movement breaks and flexible seating options, the teacher can provide James with opportunities to release his excess energy in a controlled manner, thus reducing the urge to disrupt the class by getting up frequently. This accommodation allows for an appropriate outlet for his need for movement, contributing to improved focus during seated activities.
Options A and D are not the most appropriate initial steps for addressing impulsive behaviors. Behavior charts and rewards may not address the underlying cause of impulsivity and may only provide short-term results. Referring James to the school counselor can be a valuable step, but it should come after trying environment modifications and other behavior management strategies.

QUESTION 223

Answer: C

Explanation: The best way to engage parents in the IEP development is to hold a pre-IEP meeting, commonly known as a "pre-meeting." During this meeting, the teacher can actively involve the parents in the decision-making process by discussing their concerns, preferences, and goals for their child. This collaboration helps ensure that the IEP aligns with the student's unique needs and that the parents' input is considered.
Options A and B are inappropriate approaches. Parents should be active participants in the IEP process, and excluding them from the IEP meeting or merely sending the completed IEP for their signature would not promote their involvement. Option D neglects the primary stakeholders (the parents) and should not be used as a strategy for IEP development.

QUESTION 224

Answer: C

Explanation: Recording and reviewing video footage of your classroom lessons is an effective self-assessment strategy for identifying your strengths and weaknesses as a teacher. By observing yourself teach, you can gain valuable insights into your instructional techniques, classroom management, and overall effectiveness. It allows you to reflect on your practice and make data-driven decisions to improve your teaching.

Options A and D involve seeking feedback from others, which can be helpful, but self-assessment is about reflecting on one's own practice. Option B might show the impact of the inclusive practices on students' academic performance, but it does not specifically focus on the teacher's strengths and weaknesses.

QUESTION 225

Answer: D

Explanation: The best approach for the teacher is to engage in ongoing self-reflection and learning about cultural diversity to address and mitigate potential biases. By continuously examining one's beliefs and attitudes, the teacher can develop greater cultural competence and adapt teaching strategies to better meet the needs of diverse student populations.

Options A and C are not appropriate strategies, as avoiding cultural topics or embracing biases can hinder the teacher-student relationship and negatively impact the learning environment. Option B is helpful, but the responsibility to address personal biases ultimately lies with the individual teacher.

QUESTION 226

Answer: D

Explanation: Setting goals that align with the teacher's passions and areas of interest is likely to be the most effective approach for professional growth. When teachers are personally invested in their goals, they are more motivated and dedicated to making meaningful progress in their chosen areas of improvement.

Options A and C might align with external requirements and collaboration but may not necessarily address the teacher's personal growth aspirations. Option B focuses on minimal effort and short-term goals, which may not lead to significant professional development.

QUESTION 227

Answer: C

Explanation: To improve the effectiveness of your instructional approach, it is crucial to assess the individual needs of each student and tailor your instruction accordingly. Students with learning disabilities may have varied learning styles and preferences, and adapting your approach to meet their unique needs can enhance their understanding and engagement with the material.

Options A and B may not address the root cause of the students' struggles and may not be effective in supporting their learning needs. Option D is not an appropriate solution, as it disrupts the learning environment and does not target the instructional approach itself.

QUESTION 228

Answer: A

Explanation: After identifying specific areas for growth, the teacher should create an action plan with clear, measurable goals and a timeline for improvement. This proactive approach allows the teacher to set a course of action to address the identified weaknesses and work towards enhancing their teaching practice.

Options B and C involve seeking validation from others or comparing oneself to colleagues, which may not be as productive as setting personal goals. Option D ignores the identified areas of weakness, preventing the teacher from making meaningful improvements in those areas.

QUESTION 229

Answer: A

Explanation: In an inclusive classroom, a special education teacher's main responsibility is to develop and implement specialized instructional strategies that cater to the diverse needs of students with disabilities. This involves adapting and modifying the curriculum, providing accommodations, and using various teaching techniques to ensure that all students can access and engage with the content.

QUESTION 230

Answer: B

Explanation: When a new student with a learning disability joins the class, it is essential for the special education teacher to conduct an initial assessment to understand the student's specific strengths and weaknesses. This assessment will help the teacher tailor instruction and provide appropriate support to meet the student's individual needs.

QUESTION 231

Answer: B

Explanation: If a special education teacher disagrees with the goals outlined in a student's IEP, the appropriate course of action is to consult with the school principal to request an IEP review meeting. During this meeting, the teacher can express their concerns, provide evidence or data supporting their position, and collaborate with the IEP team to make necessary adjustments to the student's goals.

QUESTION 232

Answer: C

Explanation: Collaboration between a special education teacher and a general education teacher is essential in an inclusive classroom. Both teachers should share the responsibility for planning and delivering instruction. Working together allows them to combine their expertise, knowledge, and resources to effectively address the diverse needs of all students in the class, creating a more inclusive and supportive learning environment.

QUESTION 233

Answer: C

Explanation: When a student with a specific learning disability in reading comprehension is not making significant progress despite various interventions, it is essential for the special education teacher to seek additional support and expertise. Consulting with a reading specialist or educational psychologist can help identify any underlying issues and provide more targeted and specialized interventions to address the student's specific learning needs.

QUESTION 234

Answer: C

Explanation: Ms. Johnson's realization about overlooking cultural differences is an essential step towards professional growth. To improve her instruction, she should develop a plan to incorporate culturally responsive teaching strategies. This may involve learning about her students' cultures, integrating diverse perspectives into lessons, and creating a more inclusive and supportive classroom environment.

QUESTION 235

Answer: D

Explanation: Identifying weaknesses is a crucial aspect of self-assessment. In this case, the teacher should take action to address the weakness in managing classroom behavior during transitions. Creating a behavior management plan with specific strategies for smooth and effective transitions will help improve the learning environment and student engagement.

QUESTION 236

Answer: D

Explanation: Effective professional growth requires the teacher to identify areas of improvement and set challenging, yet achievable, goals. Setting goals that are too easy may not lead to significant growth, while overly ambitious goals may result in frustration. Striking a balance between challenge and attainability encourages continuous improvement.

QUESTION 237

Answer: C

Explanation: Given that Mr. Rodriguez wants to enhance his understanding of instructional technology in the context of special education, attending workshops or webinars specifically focused on this area would be the most effective step. These specialized training sessions will offer valuable insights and practical strategies tailored to his unique teaching needs and student population.

QUESTION 238

Answer: D

Explanation: Recognizing the challenge of remaining objective in self-assessment is an important step. Enrolling in a professional development course on self-assessment and reflection will provide the necessary tools and strategies to overcome biases and improve the teacher's ability to engage in meaningful self-reflection for continued professional growth.

QUESTION 239

Answer: B

Explanation: Option B is the most effective strategy in this situation. Using a professional interpreter will ensure clear and accurate communication between the teacher and the parent. It shows respect for the parent's language and cultural background, fostering a positive and collaborative relationship. Sending written communication in English (Option A) may not be effective if the parent cannot understand the information. Requesting the parent to learn English (Option C) is not practical and may be disrespectful. Avoiding involvement (Option D) can lead to further disconnection and hinder the student's learning outcomes.

QUESTION 240

Answer: C

Explanation: Option C is the best approach for creating a positive and inclusive classroom environment. Culturally responsive teaching acknowledges and values the cultural diversity of students and incorporates it into the teaching methods and curriculum. Providing appropriate accommodations ensures that all students can access the material and participate in class activities. Segregating students with disabilities (Option A) is not inclusive and can lead to social isolation. Using standardized assessments without accommodations (Option B) may not accurately measure the abilities of diverse learners. Avoiding collaboration with parents from diverse cultural backgrounds (Option D) hinders effective communication and support for students.

QUESTION 241

Answer: C

Explanation: Option C is the most appropriate way to collaborate with parents. Involving parents in regular meetings allows them to be informed about their child's progress and challenges, while also giving them a chance to provide valuable insights. Collaborative decision-making empowers parents to actively participate in their child's education. Minimizing parental involvement (Option A) can be counterproductive and may not address the child's specific needs. Providing information only in written form (Option B) may not be accessible to the visually impaired parent. Encouraging the parents to seek support from other parents (Option D) is beneficial but should not replace direct collaboration with the teacher.

QUESTION 242

Answer: D

Explanation: Option D is the most effective strategy for promoting positive communication. Trained bilingual interpreters ensure accurate and sensitive communication between the teacher and parent, preventing misunderstandings. Relying solely on nonverbal cues (Option A) may lead to miscommunication and confusion. Using machine translation apps (Option B) can be unreliable and may result in errors in translation. Encouraging the parent to communicate in English (Option C) is not respectful of their linguistic background and may hinder effective communication.

QUESTION 243

Answer: C

Explanation: Option C is the most appropriate recommendation in this case. Providing the parent with specific strategies and resources that align with the child's learning needs can be beneficial for supporting the child's progress at home. This approach fosters collaboration between the teacher and parent and empowers the parent to play an active role in their child's education. Options A and B do not address the specific learning needs of the child, and Option D focuses on discipline rather than targeted support.

QUESTION 244

Answer: C

Explanation: Option C is the most effective method for communicating with a non-verbal student who uses AAC devices. Using the student's AAC device acknowledges their preferred mode of communication and allows them to actively participate in conversations. It shows respect for the student's abilities and ensures that their voice is heard. Options A and B do not directly involve the student with AAC in the communication process. Option D is presumptive and may overlook the student's capacity to understand and communicate.

QUESTION 245

Answer: D

Explanation: Option D is the best approach to improve communication during the conference. Checking for the parent's understanding by pausing frequently allows them to process information and seek clarifications. Providing information in a clear and accessible manner helps to avoid overwhelming the parent with complex jargon. Options A and C do not address the parent's disengagement and may hinder effective communication. Option B is helpful, but it should be combined with clear explanations during the conference to address immediate concerns.

QUESTION 246

Answer: C

Explanation: Option C is the most effective strategy for promoting collaboration between special education teachers and general education teachers. Regular meetings allow both parties to share insights, discuss individual students' needs, and develop effective strategies to support learning outcomes. Collaboration is essential in an inclusive classroom to ensure that all students receive appropriate support. Options A and D advocate for an isolated approach, which is not conducive to an inclusive environment. Option B may hinder effective collaboration as it limits the information available to general education teachers.

Milton Keynes UK
Ingram Content Group UK Ltd.
UKHW052215050923
428087UK00014B/984